BUDGIE
THE AUTOBIOGRAPHY OF GOALKEEPING LEGEND
JOHN BURRIDGE

BUDGIE

THE AUTOBIOGRAPHY OF GOALKEEPING LEGEND

JOHN BURRIDGE

with Colin Leslie

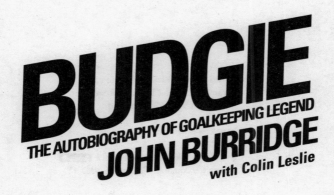

JB

JOHN BLAKE

Published by John Blake Publishing Ltd,
3 Bramber Court, 2 Bramber Road,
London W14 9PB, England

www.johnblakepublishing.co.uk

www.facebook.com/Johnblakepub facebook
twitter.com/johnblakepub twitter

First published in hardback in 2011
This edition published in 2013

ISBN: 9781857826654

British Library Cataloguing-in-Publication Data:

A catalogue record for this book is available from the British Library.

Design by www.envydesign.co.uk

Printed in Great Britain by CPI Group (UK) Ltd

1 3 5 7 9 10 8 6 4 2

Papers used by John Blake Publishing are natural, recyclable products made
from wood grown in sustainable forests. The manufacturing processes conform to
the environmental regulations of the country of origin.

Every attempt has been made to contact the relevant copyright-holders,
but some were unobtainable. We would be grateful if the appropriate people
could contact us.

CONTENTS

ACKNOWLEDGEMENTS

Thanks to all those who made this book possible, particularly the Burridge family, Scott Stevenson, David Hardie at the *Edinburgh Evening News*, the library staff at *The Scotsman*, Tim Nash at the *Express and Star* in Wolverhampton, Steve Canavan and Alison Bott at the *Blackpool Gazette*, John Wright and Sandra Kirkbride at the *Workington Times and Star*, Mel Eves, Dave Harrison, Joe Morrison, the Oman Football Association, Mike and Lillian Cooke, Andy Gray, Stevie Burns, Ashley Hammond, Allie Collins, Michelle Signore and John Blake.

AUTHOR'S NOTE

When a club has just sold the country's No.1 goalkeeper and replaced him with a veteran in his 40th year, fans can be forgiven for being a little sceptical about the new man's ability to fill the gloves. I was one of those hasty doubters in 1991, when my team Hibernian transferred Andy Goram to Rangers for £1 million and picked up John Burridge on a free transfer. I knew who Budgie was – I'd seen his animated face grinning out at me from Topps bubble gum cards throughout the seventies and eighties – but I was unaware what a larger than life character he was until I saw him prancing about his goalmouth like the oldest gazelle in town. It's safe to say Budgie was an instant hero.

The day Budgie puffed out his chest and bounced into Easter Road, Hibs had just emerged from the darkest season in a proud 116-year history. The previous summer, the owner of Edinburgh arch-rivals Hearts, Wallace Mercer, had launched a hostile takeover that would have shut the club down and ripped a famous old institution out of the community. After a bitter battle, the predator was vanquished, and Hibs were saved.

Against that backdrop season 1991/92 arrived with optimism still in short supply. However, within his 90 debut minutes, 'Budgie' had lifted the gloom and shown the fans what an incredible goalkeeper they now had at their club.

The charismatic lunatic between the goalposts was a born entertainer, and would always catch the eye with his bizarre blend of gymnastics and unbridled enthusiasm. He insisted on taking time out at the end of each game – win, lose or draw – to run to the fans to applaud their contribution, and that common touch earned him respect and admiration.

He would fully cement his place in the club's folklore by helping to lead Hibs to a fairytale League Cup success at Hampden in 1991 – barely 15 months since they had nearly been wiped off the face of the planet. The scenes that unfolded in the Scottish capital that October night as the trophy was paraded along Princes Street will never be forgotten. Not that Budgie stayed up for the party though – 'Mr Dedication' took his well-deserved bow then headed for bed after a job well done.

To this day, Budgie is widely regarded in the green half of Edinburgh as a 'legend' – a hackneyed phrase within football perhaps, but in Budgie's case no one can deny him that status.

His stay at Hibs was, of course, just one small slice of an amazing record-breaking 771-match career, spread across five decades as a player and a coach, and fans and players of the many other clubs he served will have their own memories to treasure. My own happy recollections of Budgie led me to track him down to his adopted Gulf homeland of Oman, where he works in the desert sun. He served the Oman national team as goalkeeping coach for a decade and is still going strong as a television pundit in Dubai. Budgie's antics and escapades have long popped up in the pages of team-

AUTHORS NOTE

mates' autobiographies. At last, he shares with us his own roller-coaster story which truly reflects his personality.

They say you have to be mad to be a goalie. I think Budgie might have invented that phrase.

Colin Leslie
Co-author

FOREWORD

by ANDY GRAY

What can you say about John Burridge? Oddball, crazy, madcap, loony, eccentric – Budgie's been called all of those things over the years, and laughed most of them off, but the fans absolutely loved him, his team-mates admired him and I defy you to find me a man more dedicated to football than him.

I first came across Budgie when I signed for Aston Villa in 1975. I was checking into the hotel Villa had put me in and there was Budgie waiting for me in reception, pacing the floor and hyperactive as ever. He had just signed for the club himself, and he made me very welcome as a fellow new boy. From that moment on we became pretty good friends.

We were vastly different people, but still we bonded. Both of us were focused on the same thing – making Aston Villa good and making ourselves better. We shared that common goal. But Budgie was no night owl – two halves of lager for him and he was gone. Drink didn't interest him, only football. I used to enjoy that part of football, a couple of beers with the lads, but Budgie was Mr Dedication 24/7.

Budgie would always be pushing the boundaries and thinking outside the box, to the extent that he would turn up at training wearing a big combat jacket, which had every pocket packed full with sand. It weighed a ton, but his vision was that if he wore the sand-filled jacket during training, when he took it off for games he would be floating like a butterfly and stinging like a bee. I'm not quite sure if it worked, but he would try anything if he thought it would make him a better goalkeeper. He may have been as mad as a hatter, but he was great company and single-minded about his football. Nothing got in the way of his preparations for a game – not his wife, not his kids, not anything.

I remember one infamous time he took Janet out for a date when he was courting her. He phoned her up and said: 'I'm going to take you out tonight darling.' Janet thought that would be nice, so she got on her high heels, make-up, short skirt and a jacket. When Budgie picked her up he was all wrapped up nice and warm. So off they went for their hot date...to spend a cold winter's night watching Peter Shilton! Budgie took her to a midweek game where the England keeper was playing, because he wanted to study the England No.1's every move and see if there was anything he could learn from him to make his own game better. So they stood behind the goal where Shilton was playing, with Janet shivering away in her glad rags. When half-time came, Budgie took her by the arm and said: 'Come on then, let's go' – and Janet thought to herself: 'Thank Christ for that, we're going to get something to eat and drink now.' But no, Budgie led her to the other end of the ground behind the goal Shilton would be defending in the second half. Amazingly, Janet still became his wife.

He took great pride in his performances and hated it when someone got the number one slot before him. I remember once

Jimmy Rimmer was picked ahead of him at Villa and Budgie found it really hard to take. We were practising corners at training one day and the manager Ron Saunders asked Budgie to play as an attacker – the worst thing you could possibly let him do in the circumstances – and he spent the next six or seven corners trying to smash poor Jimmy so he could get his place back.

We had some crazy times together at Villa and a lot of success too, and we were reunited a few years later at Wolves. I was already there when he joined the club and he had nowhere to stay at first, so I put him up at my house in Wolverhampton. I had a couple of big sofas that faced each other, so on a Friday night he always used to put on his gloves to get a feel for them in time for the match the following day. He would make me sit on the sofa across from him while we were watching *Coronation Street*, with a bowl of fruit in my lap, and every now and again I had to throw an apple or an orange his way to try and catch him out. He would be diving off the sofa trying to clutch these flying pieces of fruit, and that was his warm-up on a Friday night. He was just a fantastic character – in everything he did, even if some of it was a little bit bonkers.

A lot of people move away from football, but I never thought for one second that Budgie would step away from the game he is addicted to. I think he will be in football until football retires him and not the other way round. He's a one-off. He used to have me in stitches with all of his stories in the 1970s and 1980s, so he must have ten times that amount to tell now! Enjoy.

CHAPTER 1

A MATTER OF LIFE OR DEATH

'I'd gone a bit doolally and thought I'd be better off dead.'

They say that when you go mad, the men in white coats come and take you away. That's not true. It's the men in green boiler suits.

I'd been barricaded in my room for days, crying. I had persuaded myself that I had nothing to live for and suicide seemed like the best way out. It was eating away at my mind. The three o'clock buzz of playing professional football I had felt for more than 30 years had gone, and I couldn't find any substitute for that surge of adrenaline you feel coursing through your veins when it's time to run up the tunnel and hear the roar of the crowd. A 90-minute drug I had depended on was no longer there, and I was just now just plain old John Burridge, ex-goalkeeper, nearly 50. Now what was left for me?

When you stop playing it's like being a rock star whose glory days are behind him. It's hard to replace the thrill of playing and the attention you have come to depend on when it's gone. Football had been my life since I was 15, when I started off as a

£5-a-week apprentice with my home-town team Workington in the Fourth Division. I'd played at Wembley, won the Football League Cup with Aston Villa, won the Scottish League Cup with Hibs and won promotion and championships with Wolves and Crystal Palace, but now it had all gone. The game had chewed me up and spat me out. I was finding I couldn't live with football, and I couldn't live without it.

As I lay there contemplating suicide, I would occasionally hear my wife Janet knocking at the bedroom door.

'Do you want a cup of tea, John?'
'No, go away.'
'Do you want fish and chips, John?'
'No, go away.'
'Do you want some pasta, love?'
'No, go away and leave me alone. I don't want anything.'

And so it went on. I hadn't shaved, I hadn't brushed my teeth for days. I was a complete mess. I had got depression and I had got it bad. I'd been called mad often enough in my career – for walking on my hands during warm-ups, doing somersaults, sitting on the crossbar during games, having brawls with my manager, sleeping in my goalie gloves, following the same diet as African tribesmen. None of that was seen as normal behaviour, but I hadn't been mad, just 'Mr Dedication' – someone who was way ahead of his time. But this was a whole different ball game – I was in meltdown and maybe this time I *was* mad. I just wanted to crawl into a corner and die.

I was thinking about giving up on my life because I didn't have a job, I didn't have anywhere to go in the mornings, no training to go to, nothing to prepare for, and most painful of all to me was that I didn't have anywhere to go on a Saturday afternoon. If I'd been thinking clearly I would have been able to see I had plenty to live for – my wife Janet, my son Tom and my daughter Katie. But I wasn't thinking clearly; I'd gone a bit doolally and I thought I would be better off dead. I was suicidal, but mercifully Janet recognised the signs that I was about to top myself. She suggested that I should go into hospital or look for professional help to sort my head out, but I wasn't having it. I must have been so difficult to deal with. I just locked myself in the bedroom for days on end, crying.

My friends and family were worried sick about me and in desperation my wife rang Kevin Keegan – my old boss and pal from Newcastle United – and told him all about it, and how she couldn't get through to me. Between them, they decided the only way to save me from myself and get me better was to have me sectioned.

So there I was, lying on my bed in a sorry state, staring at the ceiling and thinking I might as well do everyone a favour and kill myself, when CRASH – my bedroom door came flying off its hinges and three giants in green boiler suits came wading in. I was a born fighter and there was no way I was going to come quietly, so it all kicked off. I was trying to knock hell out of them until they stuck a needle in my arse with a knock-out drug and sent me to sleep. When I woke up I was in the Priory.

At first I wanted to run away. I would have done anything to get out of that place – I was like a caged animal. Eventually, though, I got used to my medication and calmed down a bit. I was soon well enough to attend group therapy, which was a real jolt to the system. When it was my turn to say my piece, I stood up and said: 'I'm John Burridge, I'm 47 years old, I've played football all my life and I can't play any more. I'm suicidal.'

But the next person to stand up was a woman, who told us how her husband and both her children had been killed in a road accident. That was like a lightning bolt. It woke me up and put things in perspective. There were people in this world with far worse problems than me, and I felt pathetic that I was letting my problems get on top of me when this poor woman had been through far worse. Her bravery was humbling and it sent a message to me to get a grip of myself.

I decided to knuckle down and get better. I was in there for five months and I came out with a much better attitude to life. I came out full of positive thinking, but the first thing I needed to do was to get out of the UK. I had to get away from the frustration of not being able to play. I also needed to be far away from the pissing rain and the howling gales. I knew that I couldn't go to a match again because I would start crying. Some people come out of the Priory determined to give up cigarettes and alcohol. I came out of there vowing to give up English football.

I did just that, and I moved to the Middle East where I spent a decade working for the Oman Football Federation as goalkeeping coach. In many ways it was my dream job – I worked maybe 60 days a year with the national team, going to football matches and training sessions. I've been to places you can't even spell! Unfortunately, as part of a backroom team, you sometimes carry the can for the supposed mistakes of the coach, and in January 2011 the Oman FA decided to axe the head coach, Claude Le Roy, and pretty much everyone associated with him. Bloody happy new year, eh? That unfortunately included me, even though we'd been keeping a lot of clean sheets and our goalkeepers had been playing really well. It was another blow, an absolute sickener to be honest, but one I am determined to quickly bounce back from. The old

John Burridge spirit has served me well for nearly 60 years, and I'm going to need it again.

I'm not sitting on my arse feeling sorry for myself, though – I'm keeping busy as a television pundit in Dubai. It's great work if you can get it – getting paid for the privilege of watching and talking about football games from around the world. I'm keeping my mind and body active, and the world is still my oyster. There's nothing left for me in England now, but Janet and I own three houses in Muscat, and it is paradise out here in the Gulf. As I tell you my story, it's the middle of winter and I'm lying here in my hammock, gazing out at a stunning beach with the Indian Ocean beyond. Yet I still get asked whether I want to come back to England...no chance, not if I can help it! But England gave me plenty of cracking memories, and so did Scotland. I played 771 league games in Britain and had 30 clubs. Now seems as good a time as any to reflect on it all.

CHAPTER 2
'BUDGIE' HATCHES

'It was a hard upbringing. I was a man by the
age of 12. I had a chest on me that was bigger than
Marilyn Monroe's!'

I would love to tell you that I had a warm and loving upbringing, but my life as a child was absolutely horrendous. I was born on 3 December, 1961, to my mum Greta and dad Jim in Concrete Terrace, Great Clifton – a small mining village near Workington, Cumbria, in the north west of England.

My early memories of the village were of a grim landscape dominated by slag heaps – the leftover materials from down the pit. The horrible smell of sulphur was always in your nostrils and everyone led a no-frills existence. You wouldn't believe now that people lived in such harsh conditions, but there was no time for complaining. They just got on with it.

In a mining village, the men were men and the women knew their place; they kept their mouths shut or there would be hard consequences for them if they didn't. The women did all the housework and kept the family in check while the men worked hard and drank hard, my dad included. My mother was a wonderful woman who did everything she could for me and my two sisters, Lillian and Marian. My dad was the bread-winner, and like most men in the village, he was something of a hard man. Not in a way that he would throw his weight about or be a bully, it was more just a case of his harsh way of life making him that way. There was one pub in the village called the Queen's Head and that's where all the miners would drink.

I have early childhood memories of us being huddled around the radio, because we didn't have a television, and my dad would come home from the pit and if I didn't have a bath ready for him I would be in danger of getting a hiding. If you got a crack about the head or body from your dad when you were a kid, you took it like a man. If you complained, he would hit you harder. It was done to toughen you up because round these parts you had to be tough. We never had any hot running water – we used to have a washhouse and my job was to get the coal fire started, set a fire underneath a big pot filled with water and then get his bath ready for when he came home from the pit. I would have to scrub his back as he was covered in coal.

It was traditional for men in the village to go down the pit, and I was faced with the prospect that that was going to be my life too. I was taken down the pit when I was still very young to see what it was like, to give me a grounding for what was seen as my inevitable career as a miner. I watched my dad and the other miners slogging their guts out in a dark confined space with water running round them. My job was to collect all the coal and slurry he had dug out, shove it into a barrow and wheel it away.

I used to be frightened to death down there and I hated the dark. I couldn't admit that to my dad, though; he would have thought I was soft and disowned me. Mining accidents were commonplace and you would hear all the time of people dying down there. It was a very hard life. How my dad used to do it

I'll never know. They were hard, hard men. On Sundays, they would actually have fist fights outside the pub. You would see them outside, shirts off, stripped to the waist and ready to knock hell out of each other bare knuckle. It was like UFC 1960s-style – but after the punch-ups, you would see them the next day going to the pit again, comrades together, with no lingering hard feelings.

The pit may have held plenty terrors for me, but I wasn't scared of hard work. I got a job working on a farm when I was 12 and that made me grow up fast. I had to be up at 5.30 every morning, then run a mile to get there before I started getting on with my jobs. Then I had to run another mile to get the dog to help round up the cows. I was mucking in with anything that needed doing, including gathering and moving the hay bales, chopping wood, sawing wood – I wasn't the tallest kid, but my muscles and strength were developing fast with all that hard graft and I had a chest on me that was bigger than Marilyn Monroe's! I used to get a 10-shilling note every week from working on the farm. All the Burridge kids had jobs so we had an Oxo box that we used to have to put our wages in to help with the housekeeping and pay our way.

Workington wasn't really a football area. It was a big rugby league stronghold. The rugby league side, Workington Town, were a big club playing in the top division, while Workington Reds – the football team – were in the old Fourth Division and were very much in the shadow of the rugby team. Like most of the miners, my dad would always go to watch the rugby league side when they were at home. They would come out of the pit on a Friday and you would never see them again till two o'clock on Sunday for their weekly rugby game on the village green. The only time I would ever see my dad at the weekend was when he came out the pub. They used to have 15-a-side games for cash, and you wouldn't be able to play if you hadn't put your share of the kitty in. I was only 11 or 12 years old but I was playing against 18-stone miners at rugby league. We would go into the village field and wait for the miners to come out of the pub. I was wearing clogs, not football boots, because we couldn't afford them. It was 'skins' against shirts and we would play in all weather – people would take their shirts off even if it was snowing. I remember one game when my dad was in the opposite side to me. He was a good player and a good athlete. I saw him coming towards me, and there was no question of him going easy on me. SMASH, he battered right into me and scored. He took the money, went straight into the pub, with not even the slightest remorse that his boy was outside with a black eye. There was no mollycoddling, but I wouldn't change it for anything. Playing with the miners was hardening me up, and it stood me in good stead when I played with lads of my own age, because it seemed far easier by comparison. It was a hard, hard upbringing. I was a man by the age of 12.

I enjoyed rugby, but football was always my main passion, and for some reason I always wanted to be a goalkeeper. I don't why, but I was just attracted to the one position that made you stand out from the crowd. I was a born showman. The field in the village was kept like a bowling green and you would find me and my mates down there most days kicking a ball about. When I go home now I'll drive past that field, but you never see anyone playing football there now which is sad. I was the most popular lad in the village because every Christmas my dad used to give me a leather ball because I was always playing football. If I wasn't in the football field during daytime, I was in the Miners' Welfare boxing. I was a good boxer and I could look after myself. I was always fighting older lads. I was in the Cumbrian YMCA under-16 championship at Carlisle when I was 14, fighting lads who were 16; another thing that really toughened me up.

I was playing rugby one week, football the next, and boxing in between. At 13 years old I was playing for the Workington district team, and I also later played for England schoolboys at rugby, second row. At 13, I was playing football with 16-year-olds – they were all big but I was a little hard nut, and I was an athlete, because I was so strong from working on the farm. We had a very good district team. We had a lad called Dave Irving, who played for Workington and then Everton, and Peter Nicholson, who started off at Blackpool and went on to play hundreds of games for Bolton. I got noticed playing for our district team and then made the progression into the Cumbria area team, where we would play against the likes of Scotland, Yorkshire and Lancashire, with our home games taking place at Carlisle. Scouts were starting to watch my games and I was getting noticed. It was only a matter of time before a club came calling.

To be honest I was very ashamed of my house. There were no indoor toilets in those days, and our lavvy, like every other house round our way, was outside. If you wanted to go during the night, we had these quaint things we called 'piss pots', which would be kept under the bed for emergencies. Rather than walk across the yard in the snow in the middle of the night you would just forget about dignity and use one of those. They put flowers in them now and you see them being sold in antique shops, but they had a more practical use when I was kid. Unluckily for me, I was the one given the job of emptying the piss pots in the morning. I love the smell of piss in the morning! It wasn't exactly the perfect way to start your day, that's for sure. My dad had a novel approach when the piss pot was full – and after downing a few drinks, he would come in drunk and with his bladder full of ale and at bursting point, so he would be needing to go a few times during the night. But there's no way he was going to stumble outside into the yard to use the toilet, instead he would just piss into the pot then chuck the contents out the window. It would go splashing all over the yard outside. Or, if he had really had a skinful and even that was too much trouble, he'd just open the window and piss straight out into the yard.

It was shameless the way we lived, but I suppose that's how you find footballers – a lot of them came from that kind of working-class background. You talk about favelas in Brazil, but a favela in Brazil looked like a five-star hotel next to my house. I was brought up in such a harsh way. The conditions and the squalor were horrendous. As I said, we had no hot water and when I came in from playing football or rugby I would have to do my own washing, and often my kit wouldn't dry out in time for my next match.

So when I started getting noticed playing football, people would be coming up to me after games and asking where I was from and where I lived, but I was a bit ashamed to tell them. Finally one day somebody took the plunge and turned up at my house unannounced. The first manager to set foot on the Burridge family pile was Tony Waddington, the famous manager of Stoke City, who signed Gordon Banks and later Peter Shilton, and won Stoke the League Cup in 1972. He obviously knew a good goalkeeper when he saw one! Waddington had driven all the way from Stoke to Workington, and we saw his big car pull up at the end of the drive.

As courtesy demanded back then, before he could sign me he had come to speak with me and my dad about the possibility of me joining Stoke, who were one of the bigger clubs of the day. But when you were an apprentice professional in those days, it didn't matter if you went to Manchester United or a Fourth Division team – your weekly wage was £5 regardless. It was all regulated by the FA, to stop the big clubs cherry-picking all the best young players, and to give the others a chance of operating on a level playing field.

We had never seen a big car like his, so there was quite a buzz in the house as he pulled up, with everyone looking to see who it was. It had been a wash day and we had all the wet washing hanging up in the yard to dry on the wash lines. You could see Waddington fighting his way through the washing to make his way to our door, but after year on year of my dad pissing in the yard it had become a treacherous, slimy surface, and he slipped when he reached the middle of my dad's target area, and went down like a sack of spuds, slap bang on his arse. His brand new Prince of Wales checked suit was covered in piss. It was so embarrassing, you could see the look of disbelief on his face as he put his hand to his nose to smell what he had slid in, and then had his worst fears confirmed.

He came into the house all flustered and smelling of piss, asking: 'What the hell is that?' My dad had been out for a few beers, and was sitting there rolling a cigarette, and he barely looked up as he demanded: 'Who are you, like?' My dad didn't know him from Adam. I didn't know who he was, because we didn't have a television and the only footballers and managers I knew were the ones I'd seen in my Charlie Buchan magazines. To his credit, he composed himself and replied: 'My name is Tony Waddington, I'm the manager of Stoke City Football Club. I've been watching your son play and I would like him to sign for us.'

My dad didn't beat about the bush and asked straight out how much they would be paying me. Waddington told him £5 a week, same as any other club. Without a moment's pause, my dad told him to fuck off. My dad wanted me to play for

Workington rugby league team, because they were showing interest in me as well. He reckoned I could earn £10 down the pit and a further £10 playing for Workington – £20 a week, which in those days was an awful lot of money for a lad just coming out of school. My dad had already told me he didn't want me playing football because he thought it was a 'poofs' game'. This poor fella had just driven hundreds of miles from Stoke, got covered in piss, and my dad had sent him packing with two brutal words.

The next to have a crack at signing me were Blackpool, but they got the same treatment from my old man. I was in despair and I was sitting on the stairs crying my eyes out when my mum saw me and asked: 'What's up?' I told her how much I wanted to be a footballer and that I didn't want to play rugby or go down the pit.

A few weeks later, it was the turn of my local club Workington Reds to try their luck. The manager Bobby Brown came to the house, and said he was aware that other clubs had been keen to sign me. He made a really strong case based on the benefits of signing for my local club, including being able to stay at home. My dad was just about to give him the usual response straight to his face, but then amazingly my poor old mum stepped in. You have to remember that in those days women had to mind their own business. If they opened their mouth they would most likely get a crack in the face. You wouldn't even get done for assault in those days if it was a domestic matter between husband and wife; that was just the way it was. If you were a woman, you did the washing, you did the cooking, and your reward was respect, but nothing more. So it took all the guts in the world for my mum to speak up. 'Jim, maybe we should let him sign?' she said. My first thought was: 'Oh, mum, what have you done? You are going to get the biggest black eye in the world!' God bless her, I'm in tears now recalling the moment. I thought she was going to get battered. I will remember her selflessness and unbelievable bravery to my dying day. But thankfully my dad was in a good mood that day and he listened to what she was saying. He turned to me and said: 'You've got a year. If you don't make it you're going down the pit to earn a real living.' I had one year to prove that I could play.

I thought: 'Brilliant – I'm signing for my home-town club.' I was so excited. I couldn't believe my luck and kept expecting my dad to go crazy and have a change of heart, but he was quite relaxed about it. So Workington took me down to their ground, Borough Park, the next day and said: 'Here's your contract, son'. I had three or four weeks before I could leave school but on the day I left I ran right down to the football ground at four o'clock; I just couldn't wait to get my football career started. It wasn't an easy job though. Every day at Workington I had to be there at nine o'clock because I was the only apprentice on the books. I had 30 professionals to look after – that meant there were 30 pairs of boots to clean, 30 jerseys to look after, 30 pairs of shorts, plus I had to mop the dressing rooms, absolutely scrub them. I'd be there at nine o'clock, hang everything out, make sure the boots were clean, then the players would start coming in from 9.30. One of them started calling me 'Budgie' – I've no idea where it came from, but it stuck. Maybe it's because I was flying up and down doing jobs for them. I was only 15, but I would go out and train alongside them and they would treat me with respect – it was a fantastic grounding. There were only two goalkeepers at the club and, while I was in the reserves, I would be involved in all the training games with the senior pros in the first team. I also got my first pair of brand new boots! Everything I had ever played in up until that point was hand-me-down. In the past, I had always been given boots that my dad had found me, or old ones he'd played rugby in – even when I'd played for the schoolboy select teams – painted black. But now I finally had my first pair of 'trendies', a handsome pair made by Adidas.

CHAPTER 3

ONE GAME DOWN, 770 TO GO

*'Signing for Workington and becoming an apprentice
footballer at the age of 16 may have been an exciting
prospect, but there was no glamour in it. How could
there be when we were toiling away in the depths of
the old Fourth Division?'*

To begin with, I was playing in youth team and reserve
games, and just keeping my head down and trying to make
a positive impression. My first-team breakthrough, when it
came at the end of the 1968/69 season, was totally unexpected.
There was no big build-up, it just happened. I'd just walked a
mile from my house and was waiting on the bus to take me to
Sunderland for a reserve game, and as I was waiting the
manager pulled up in his car, rolled down the window and said
to me: 'You're not going to Sunderland today son...you're
playing for the first team.'

We were lying mid-table and that day we were playing
Newport County, who were third from bottom. My head was
spinning with excitement as he took me back the 10 miles into
Workington in his big Ford Zephyr 4 car. It was still hours before
kick-off, so I just sat there in the boiler room from half past ten
till about half past one when the players started coming in. There
wasn't even much opportunity to feel nervous because before the

game, as part of my apprentice duties, I had to help get the dressing rooms ready and mark the pitch with the groundsman Billy Watson. Billy wasn't one for soft-soaping you and treating you with the kid gloves; he treated you like a man and made you work like one too. One day, before our first game of the season, he was so pleased with his handiwork that he wanted a photo of the pitch, looking all lush and green like a bowling green, so he handed me an old camera and told me to climb up the floodlight pylon to take the picture. I was terrified of heights, but he told me 'If you don't get your arse up there, I'll make sure you get the sack!'

He was quite a character and had been great pals with Workington's former manager, the great Bill Shankly, who had wanted to take him to Anfield as groundsman there. But Billy stayed at Workington to look after his mother. Shankly hadn't been the only great former Reds manager; Ken Furphy had been there in the early 1960s, and it was him who had signed the man I was about to displace as No.1, Mike Rogan – a goalkeeper I was able to learn a lot from. He played more than 400 times for Workington, so he was the perfect guy to look up to in terms of his experience.

But he'd picked up an injury and it was me and not him who would be in goal that day against Newport. There I was, sitting there an hour before kick-off, about to play the first of 771 games in my career. The older pros were doing their best to make me feel at ease, but there were 11,500 people in the ground and it was impossible to keep the nerves at bay. Newport had a big lump of a centre-forward, well over six feet, and when they took an in-swinging corner he got in front of me and scored at the near post. I couldn't believe it – their first corner of the game and I'd already let one in. I was feeling a bit out my depth, thinking to myself, 'My God, what am I doing here?' But we equalised, and then we went 2-1 in front. They equalised again, but to my relief we won the game 3-2. It wasn't a fantastic debut by any stretch of the imagination. I hadn't done very well and I got a bit of stick for it. Welcome to professional football.

But Mike was still out injured and I was the only other keeper they had, so it didn't matter how I'd played, I would be in at the deep end again. Every team, especially in the harsh environment of the Fourth Division, had a big centre-forward in those days who would be used as a battering ram. They used to do their best to put the fear of death up goalkeepers, and while I wasn't scared of them, I did learn some hard lessons playing against some of those grizzled old campaigners. I remember we had a midweek game against Oldham, and they had a centre-forward called Jim Fryatt, who had a reputation for being an intimidating character. He was bald and on a wet day you could hear the ball slap off his head. The local paper had been suggesting John Burridge was too inexperienced to be playing against an old warhorse like Fryatt, who was built like a brick shithouse and could dish out some harsh treatment. It was a big game for us, because Oldham had just been relegated the season before from the Third Division, and they were seen as the big boys of the league and the team that everyone wanted to beat.

It was a horrible wet and windy Tuesday night, and they slung everything in for big Jim Fryatt. I may have been 16, but that didn't matter to him – he was an assassin in football boots. If I was old enough to play, I was old enough to take whatever punishment he felt like dishing out. First chance he got, he came steaming in and broke my nose. There was blood everywhere. My nose was all over the place, and my eyes were stinging, but what I would in time refer to as the 'John

Burridge spirit' kicked in and the broken nose just made me even more determined to succeed. I made save after save and I played a blinder. With five minutes left, we scored and won it 1-0. The manager ran on to the field and picked me up, shouting: 'That was brilliant, son.' I must have lost half a pint of blood out of my nose. The papers the next day had changed their tune after giving me some stick on my debut. They were now saying that I could be the next Gordon Banks and hailing a fantastic performance from the plucky 16-year-old who had stood up to big bad Fryatt.

These big centre-forwards used to do everything they could to mash you up, but I never held any grudges. It was a man's game, and all those hard knocks were part of my education. It was the making of me, and it only helped to toughen me up. So, to Jim Fryatt, I suppose I should say thank you for breaking my nose and preparing me properly for a life in football. Another game that sticks in the mind was an away trip to Southport where I was up against a fella called Eric Redrobe. He also had a reputation for being a bit of a hard man, and at corner kicks he would be growling under his breath that he was going to kill you. True to his word, he hammered into me and broke my rib. I was in absolute agony. I was still recovering from the smashed nose, and now I had a cracked rib to add to the broken bones collection. But again the never-say-die spirit kicked in. There were no substitute goalkeepers, so I just had to get on with it. I played on and had a good game and we won, so I was starting to believe in the philosophy 'no pain, no gain'. If I had any broken bones, strains or bruises, they would just strap me up for each game and let me get on with it. I was young, strong and a quick healer. To me, getting a few bumps and bruises was just an occupational hazard. I was loving it. I was also driven by the constant threat hanging over my head that if the football didn't work out, my dad would make me play rugby and work down the pit – that was all the motivation I needed to stick at it and be a success.

Although I was keeping Mike Rogan out of the team, there was never any danger of me getting ideas above my station. Whatever I did out on the pitch on a Saturday, I was still just a £5-a-week apprentice and the only way to survive at a club like Workington was hard graft and showing plenty of respect to your elders. I may have been playing every week, but I was still the dogsbody and I had plenty of jobs to do around the ground. After the home games, even though I'd just been playing myself, I had to run down to the opponents' dressing room with a brush and sweep all the mud that had come from the players' boots into a corner so they didn't get their feet dirty when they stepped out of the bath. I would come down with my kit still on, and they would do a double-take when they saw me standing there and ask: 'Haven't you just been playing in goal for them?' After I'd done my bit in the away dressing room the manager used to make me pick up and sort out all the kit in our dressing room. I had to make sure the jerseys weren't inside out, then put all the red shirts together, gather the white shorts in another big tub full of soap powder, and pick up all the red stockings and stick them in another container. Next, I had to sweep out the home dressing room. When I'd done all that, I could finally have a bath myself, but I still had to cycle the 10 miles home. By the time all my duties had finished and I'd cycled home on my bike it could be about half past ten and all I was ready for was sleep.

My father was no fan of football, and when I first made the breakthrough I got no obvious signs of encouragement from him. I didn't want to start crowing about it in case he took that for me being a cheeky bugger and shut me up in the easiest possible way – by telling me that I could go and work down the pit like him.

I used to get two complimentary tickets for each game and I'd sometimes ask my dad if he wanted to come down and watch me, but his response was always a fairly blunt: 'I'm not coming to watch bloody football – it's a poofs' game.' He had his set routine each weekend – he'd have a skinful on a Friday night and keep drinking in the pub till the Sunday. The rugby team would be at home one week, and the football team the next, and while he would usually head down to see the rugby boys in action, he didn't pay much attention to how I was getting on with Workington Reds...or so I thought.

There was a home game against Southport and during the match one of their forwards caught me flush in the face. I could feel his studs raking right into my forehead as I dived at his feet. I was out cold briefly, and as I came back to my senses, I became vaguely aware of a figure lurching towards the forward that had just booted me. Then it hit me – it was me dad on the pitch, making towards the penalty box...with a pint pot in his hand. He'd been on the piss since Friday night – by this time it was about 4.15 on the Saturday and he was well and truly the worse for wear.

He headed right for the bewildered forward, shouting at him: 'You! You big bugger! Pick on someone your own bloody size. C'mon and fight me!' He then swung an arm and threw his beer all over the guy. All hell broke loose and the two of them got into a fight. I was a bit groggy from the boot in the face, and I thought I had concussion or something because, unless my eyes were playing tricks on me, my old dad was on the pitch fighting with Southport's centre-forward.

The next thing I knew the police came on to the pitch, got a hold of my dad, and arrested him. I'd snapped out of my daze, realising it wasn't a dream, and I started screaming at the coppers: 'Leave 'im. It's me dad!' In the end they just threw him out of the ground instead of arresting him and chucking him in the cells and that was the end of the matter. There were no TV cameras, so there was no need for any inquest or fuss after the game. Football was a working-class game and nobody got on their high horse.

I wouldn't have let him know it, because there wasn't much in the way of outward displays of emotion in the Burridge household, at least not where my dad was concerned, but I was just secretly chuffed that he'd been at the game in the first place. It said a lot for his principles too, that he would rather pay to get in than take a complimentary ticket from me. I spoke to a few of his mates, and it turned out he'd been there before shouting encouragement, so even though he didn't show it, he must have been proud to watch his boy in goal for the Reds.

I wasn't ashamed at all that my dad had waded in that day, sticking up for his boy, but there was no hiding my shame and embarrassment when I did perhaps THE most stupid thing of my career in another game.

We were playing against Southend and coasting along towards full-time, five or six-nil up. I had had very little to do in the game, and my concentration wasn't fully switched on. I was getting a bit bored and just wanted to hear the final whistle and get in for a bath to warm myself up, so I turned round and asked the photographer sitting behind the goals how long there was left to play. He checked his watch and told me we were already well into time added on. A minute later, our full-back passed the ball back to me, and I picked it up then started bouncing it and rolling it around the box, just trying to run down the final couple of seconds. He obviously thought there was time for us to get another goal and was screaming at me: 'Budgie, Budgie, give me the ball back!' But I wasn't paying him much attention. I then heard the whistle, and as I turned round to get my cap and gloves from the back of the net I threw the ball up and volleyed it as hard as I could into the net. It was only when I turned round that I realised I had made a terrible mistake. The referee was signalling for a goal and trotting up towards the halfway line. It hadn't been him who had blown the whistle; it had been some joker in the crowd with another whistle. Our full-back was on the floor laughing his head off. We might have won the game 5-1, but after the game the manager went crazy at me. He didn't really see the funny side. I was mortified at my mistake and just kept shaking my head, trying to say sorry and pointing out that it didn't really matter – we had won the game easily anyway.

I wasn't the only one in the team who was as daft as a brush, though. I remember after one game we'd lost, the manager was going crackers at us all, shouting and swearing his head off. He picked on John Ogilvie, and pointed to his club badge and said: 'You've no idea what that badge stands for'. John was having a fag, as a lot of players did in those days, and he looked him up and down, staring at the big badge that said 'WAFC'. He casually took a drag of his ciggy and said: 'Of course I know what it stands for – "What A Fucking Football Club"!'

I had a few managers at Workington, even though I was only there a relatively short time. First there was Bobby Brown and then Frank Upton, and I didn't always see eye-to-eye with the man who eventually sold me, Brian Doyle, who took over from Frank in 1968. Brian had been known as a bit of a hardman as a player, but my first impressions of him were not good. He came into the dressing room all surly and told us:

'I'm the boss, if anyone wants to argue, come behind the stand with me now and we can sort it out.' There were a lot of experienced professionals in that dressing room, and it didn't matter that they were Fourth Division players, they deserved far better treatment than that. It's not the way to get a team pulling together, and his management style was only going to get him nowhere fast. He was the boss, and I respected that. I had no problem with those in authority, but I couldn't take anyone trying to pick on me. It wasn't in my nature.

We used to play training games on an ash pitch and on Fridays he used to join in with the five-a-sides. I was already wary of him, but when he came charging into me in goal, I blocked him the best I could then smacked him with the ball right in the face. I didn't say anything. I just did it. He got up and you could see he was starting to lose his head, but he didn't want to make a big issue of it and lose face in front of the rest of the lads, who were loving every minute of this young upstart putting the bully boy in his place. They were shouting: 'Go on Budgie son, give him some more!' I would have fought him no problem if it had come down to it. I always had that aggression from my upbringing, and my boxing. So if somebody banged me in the nose I was going to react. It didn't come to that, but you could see him seething with rage, and I was always watching my back when he was around.

My Workington days were very harsh but it was a great grounding to start a career in professional football. It gave me a chance to play at a very early age that I would not have got anywhere else. I picked up so much invaluable experience from the older professionals. If I had signed for one of the big clubs, then I would have trained every day with kids my own age, and been kept separate from the first team. At Workington, everyone trained together, and I quickly grew up and started to get a lot of confidence. I may have been wet behind the ears for that first game against Newport County, but I soon found my belief and discovered how to protect myself against the seasoned professionals you found in the Fourth Division. You only get experience by playing and learning from any mistakes you make. I could have gone to someone like Manchester United but I would never have been picking up that type of experience. I'd come a long way since that first game in a short space of time.

CHAPTER 4
BLACKPOOL ROCKS

*'No more Southport and Southend United,
now it would be Manchester United and Arsenal.
I was about to leap up three divisions in the
blink of an eye.'*

When my dad died, I was almost fined for it by Workington. Even though I was by now playing for the first team, I was still expected to turn out for youth and reserve games, and on the day my dad died we were due to play a fixture against Bradford Park Avenue. I went to the house to get my stuff for the game, but when I got there I was told not to come in; my mum was in a right old state and her friends broke the news to me that my dad had dropped dead.

Because I hadn't turned up in time for the Bradford game, the manager was blazing mad with me, saying he was going to fine me. But when I explained to him what had happened, both he and the club couldn't have been more helpful. He didn't fine me, of course, and he really helped my mum cope with the grief. The club told my mum that if there was anything they could do for the family, they would do it. The club helped with the funeral, the ceremony and all the arrangements for the crematorium. I was just a young kid and wouldn't have known where to start with the arrangements, even though I was now the man of the house. The boss and all the players came to the funeral to lend me support, which meant a lot to me. I suppose I could have taken time off, but in my mind I had to keep playing; it was the best way to cope with the situation. I knew that if I wasn't playing then Mike Rogan would be straight back in the team, and if he played well then the gloves would be his again and it would be my turn to kick my heels and wait for my chance to get back in. It was a harsh outlook perhaps, but I needed to be harsh on myself if I wanted to be a success.

We had to move out of the pit house simply because my dad wasn't working down the mine anymore, so we moved out of Concrete Terrace and into a council house in Workington – which was absolutely great, because for the first time in our lives we had hot running water. It's a horrible thing to say, but my dad dying worked out well for us as a family. We were all relieved to move away from the slag heaps, the pollution and the disgusting smell of sulphur. That council house in Workington felt like a mansion after where we'd been. We actually felt quite posh, because although we might not have admitted it to outsiders, we had been ashamed of the previous house.

Not long after that, I was told after a youth game that the manager wanted to see me. I was thinking to myself: 'What the hell have I done now? I'm going to get a bollocking here...' But he didn't beat about the bush. 'I've sold you for £20,000 and you're going to Blackpool tomorrow,' he informed me.

'What if I don't want to go?' I asked, briefly trying to protest. But it was pointless. He said the club needed the money, and that it was already a done deal. They had Mike Rogan, so it made financial sense for a skint club like Workington Reds to offload me and get some money while they could. If I'd stopped and thought about it, it was a no-brainer. Blackpool were in the First Division – I would be mixing it with the big boys. No more Southport and Southend United; now it would be Manchester United and Arsenal. I was about to leap up three divisions in the blink of an eye.

I may have been a 17-year-old kid, but the Blackpool manager, Bob Stokoe, didn't see signing me as a gamble. He'd seen me play while he was manager of Carlisle United and knew what I could do. Blackpool had gone through a lot of managers in the years before Stokoe was appointed and were proving to be a bit of a yo-yo club, bouncing between the First and Second Divisions. When I signed, Bob Stokoe was only just in the door at Bloomfield Road himself, and again Blackpool were heading for relegation to the Second Division. He had decided that the best way to give the club a chance of bouncing back at the first attempt would be to go for a rebuilding strategy of out with the old and in with the new.

They were living on past glories a bit, having famously won the FA Cup in 1953 back in the days of Stanley Matthews, but there was no doubting they were still a big club with some top players. I had the butterflies when I got to the ground for the first time to sign my contract and was shown into reception. I sat there waiting for what seemed like eternity, then all of a sudden a door opened and Stokoe said: 'Come in, John.' He was very businesslike about it, and the figures he started chucking at me were mind-blowing to a kid who had been living on a fiver a week at Workington. He said: 'Right son, we've agreed a £20,000 transfer. Your salary will be £55 a week with £45 appearance money if you play in the first team. We'll also give you a £1,000 signing-on fee and your mother will receive £30 every month sent to her in a cash envelope.' I couldn't believe it – £100 a week, it sounds laughable now, but that was beyond my wildest dreams. All I could bring myself to blurt out was: 'Can I phone my mam?'

We didn't have a phone in our house so I had to phone the pub round the corner in Workington and ask them to go and get Mrs Burridge from down the road. The barman went round and fetched her and she was on the other end of the phone five minutes later – it was the first time she'd ever set foot in a pub. When I told her I'd be getting £100 a week the phone went dead – I thought she'd died on the spot of a heart attack! She was so shocked. I was doing all the sums in my head and thought I had won the lottery. There was no more time to mess around. I went back to see Bob Stokoe and told him I'd sign a four-year contract.

Blackpool found me accommodation in a boarding house not far from the ground. There were other kids my age staying there, but they were apprentices on £5 a week, while I was on a £100 a week as a first-team player. It was all over the local paper that I'd signed, but there was no Billy Big Time about me. I got on well with the other lads, as we were all about the same age. It was strange being away from home and I didn't really have any clothes to my name. I had a skinhead in those days and my entire wardrobe consisted of a pair of bovver boots, two pairs of pants, a checked shirt and a skinhead suit. It was a giant boarding house and the landlady used to do all the cooking. I spent most of the time in my room or in the television room. I was happy with my move there, not at all homesick, and it was an exciting time in my life to be out of home and out at last in the big, wide world.

My first day at training was a bit of an eye-opener as the squad was packed with big names in football. I had already heard all about Jimmy Armfield, who used to be the England captain and was something of a club legend, but there were other strong characters like Glyn James, the Welsh international centre-half, and the Scottish internationals Tony Green and Tommy Hutchison.

I didn't have to wait long for my debut, and it was a daunting one – away to Everton, who were known as the 'Bank of England' club because of the amount of cash they'd splashed on signings during that era. They were a top side, and had won the league in 1970, so for an introduction to the First Division it was about as big as it could get. I got a good night's sleep before the game, and was told to report to Bloomfield Road the next morning to catch the team bus to the game. I didn't even know where Everton was – I thought it was down south somewhere, so it was a bit of a surprise when we set off towards Liverpool.

Like I said, I didn't have much of a wardrobe, so my outfit for the day was a checked shirt, bovver boots and a turquoise suit. I even had to borrow a tie off one of the apprentices because I didn't have one. As soon as I got on to the coach, Tommy Hutchison and Tony Green – who were the real jokers of the team – started taking the piss out of me something terrible. All the rest of the team were dressed like professionals in their blazers and flannels, and I stood out like a turquoise sore thumb. I was almost crying with embarrassment. I was squirming on my seat all the way there as Tony and Tommy absolutely slaughtered me about my gear. I just wanted to go home and I had the right hump with them. They may have been experienced professionals, but if they'd kept pushing my buttons I would have gladly fought them all and broken their noses!

When we got to Goodison it was a relief to get the suit off and into my kit. I was a little bit nervous, but as soon as I went down the tunnel and over that white line all the anxiety disappeared and the adrenaline took over. There were 46,000 people inside Goodison, it was my first game in the First

Division and I knew everything I did would be scrutinised, but I played an absolute blinder. It couldn't have gone better. One ball from the left wing came over and Everton's star striker Joe Royle hit it on the volley, sweet as a nut, and I held it. I'd been used to playing against the journeymen of the Fourth Division and here I was facing a team full of internationals, but I wasn't frightened of them whatsoever. I'd never seen any of them before, so for me there was nothing to fear. They were just guys in blue shirts. In my mind, it wasn't about what they did, it was down to how I played and handled the occasion.

Brian Labone, another England international who had just played at the World Cup in Mexico, also went close for Everton late on, but again I saved it, and we battled to a 0-0 draw. When I got back into the dressing room everybody was patting me on the back and saying well done. Some of the lads said they would be buying me a drink in the players' lounge, but as soon as I'd had my bath I got my dreaded suit on and headed straight for the bus where I lay down on the back seat, hiding. I couldn't stand the thought of attracting any more flak for what I was wearing, especially not in a packed players' lounge full of internationals.

After about an hour, the team started coming back on to the bus from the players' lounge. Bob Stokoe came over to me and congratulated me again on a great game, and asked for me for more of the same in the next game against Manchester United. But his face dropped when I told him: 'I'm not playing. I'm going home.' He could see I was upset about something and when I pointed to Tommy Hutchison and Tony Green and told him they'd been taking the piss out of my suit, Stokoe went down the bus to have a quiet word with them. Tommy came up a couple of minutes later, arms out apologetically, and said: 'C'mon Budgie, we were only pulling your leg. We just wanted you to feel like one of the lads,' but I still had the hump and told him to sod off.

I lightened up a bit as the journey wore on; it was hard not to because everyone was full of praise for the way I'd played and making me feel like a million dollars. When we arrived back in Blackpool, they said: 'C'mon you're coming out with us tonight fox-hunting – after the game you've had there's no way you're going home.' The radio reports had also been raving about my performance, so in the space of five or six hours I'd gone from wanting to crawl into a corner to die with embarrassment at my skinhead suit to thinking I'd turned into Superman – I was getting totally swept away by all the euphoria. Blackpool was just as lively for nightlife then as it is now, and playing for the local team made you something of a local hero when you were out. People didn't really know who I was yet, because I'd just joined, but all the other lads were getting plenty of attention, especially from the ladies.

I'd had a couple of pints of beer and because I'd never really drunk before I was pissed out my brains, strutting my stuff on the dance floor like a man possessed. A woman took a shine to me and started dancing with me, and when she told me: 'You're coming home with me tonight,' I wasn't in any position say no. We got a taxi back to her place and she made it plain what she was expecting from me. She was all over me the moment the front door clicked shut and in the heat of passion we moved over to the settee. She lay back on the settee, so I knelt down and tried to get myself into position. Within seconds, I told her I'd finished, but it wasn't her I'd been gyrating against – I'd been having my first sexual encounter with the cushion of the settee. I was cringing with embarrassment that I'd shagged a sofa! I suppose I can't have been that embarrassed by the incident, mind you, because it was always a good story to pull out of the locker as an ice-breaker when I was getting to know new team-mates later in my career – I don't think it ever failed to get a laugh.

The Sunday newspapers used to give players marks out of 10, and to my delight I saw I had got 10 out of 10 for my performance at Everton, even if it was probably a zero out of 10 for my sexual prowess. However, the girl in question wasn't too put off by my bungling attempts to be Casanova. I spent the next night with her too and, keeping well away from the cushions this time, I lost my virginity. I was starting to grow up, starting to become a man.

At training during the week, I was told the manager wanted to see me. I went to his office and sat outside thinking he wanted to haul me over the coals about my night out clubbing, or something else I'd done that I couldn't remember from my drunken Saturday night. Instead he told me to come with him because we were going for a drive. He took me down to Blackpool town centre and said he wanted to help me to start looking like a footballer. He got me two pairs of grey flannels, two blazers, some nice ties, five shirts, stockings and a pair of shiny shoes. 'We've got Manchester United next and I want to see a performance,' he told me. 'Now you can look the part on and off the pitch.' That was brilliant, a great gesture by him, and I felt so smart.

In the build-up to the match, I was getting all sorts of advice on how to play against George Best – folk telling me to stand up when he was running through and not to let him make my mind up for me. All my friends from Workington were big Manchester United fans and were coming down to see the game. They wanted me to get autographs from Bobby Charlton and George Best and all the other United stars, so I took their autograph books and said 'No problem'.

Wearing my blazer and flannels, I may have looked like a footballer, but I was still just an excited football-mad boy at heart and two hours before the game I was standing outside the ground with my pals' autograph books, getting George Best and Bobby Charlton to sign them. The Manchester United team coach pulled up, and there I was – looking like just another star-struck fan to them – saying: 'Will you sign this, Mr Charlton, please? Will you sign that, Mr Best?' I would be out on the pitch playing against them in an hour, but here I was bowing and scraping to them like they were my idols!

My friends had all gathered behind the goal and I could hear them giving me stick and cheering on United – so much for getting behind their mate and encouraging him in the biggest game of his career so far. Instead, I could hear them shouting: 'Hey Budgie, they are going to put five past you!' But that was all I needed to spur me on – I was ready for battle, and there was no way I was going to embarrass myself with them watching my every move. When United got their first corner, Bobby Charlton looked me up and down and recognised me from outside the ground. 'Didn't I just sign an autograph for you? That's never happened to me before!' he laughed. From another corner, we went 1-0 down. The ball was bouncing around the box like a pinball, before it fell to the deadly boot of Denis Law who stuck it in the net. After that, though, I came into my own and was magnificent. I saved what would have been a certain goal in the top corner, then we equalised just before half-time. When we changed ends at half-time, all my mates were behind me again. I didn't mind anyone else giving me stick, but to hear the mates I'd been to school with dishing out the abuse riled me. I was game for anything. All the words of advice I had been given about George Best started rushing through my mind when I saw him running through, with just me to beat. I was thinking to myself, 'Stand up to him, stand up to him', so I held my ground till the last second, and when he feinted to take the ball round to my right, I went down at his feet with all I could muster, and took the ball cleanly. As I smothered the ball, I could feel him hurtling over the top of me, and as I got up I could hear him a few yards away screaming like a pathetic little girl: 'Aghhh my foot!' I had the ball in my hands, and completely forgetting the football God, idolised by millions, that was lying in front of me, I started ranting and raving at him: 'You poof, get up.' I knew he was a superstar, but there I was berating him and telling him: 'Next time you run through, I'll make sure I break your leg, now fuck off out of my box.' It wasn't big and it wasn't clever to say something like that to somebody as classy as George Best, but I was just carried away with the moment and the adrenaline had kicked in and taken over my mouth. I had been getting his autograph just a couple of hours earlier, but here I was doing my best to sort him out on the football pitch. To be fair to Georgie, he just got up, gave me a funny sideways look as if I had just beamed down from another planet, and got on with the game. The match finished 1-1, a creditable result for Blackpool against such famous opponents, and it took me a while to come down after that. I made sure my so-called mates were put in their place too – even Manchester United couldn't beat Budgie that day! What a buzz I got from the experience – I was desperate for more.

CHAPTER 5
THE ITALIAN JOB

*'I'd never even been on an aeroplane before –
Budgie was about to get his wings!'*

I had settled very well into my role as a First Division footballer, and was enjoying every minute of Blackpool. It had been great playing against the superstars of that day like Martin Chivers and Alan Gilzean of Tottenham and Bobby Charlton and George Best of Manchester United. Every week held something different, and it was a far cry from my baptism into football at Workington.

I'd only just turned 18 and I still had my £1,000 signing-on fee sitting in the bank. I hadn't needed to touch it. I was averaging more than £100 a week and in 1971 terms that was decent money for a teenager. But the club was heading for the Second Division. We'd only won four out of 42 games, and although the writing was on the wall long before Stokoe took over, we finished bottom of the heap. There was no time for moping about relegation, though, because in the summer of 1971 Blackpool embarked on one of their greatest and most glorious adventures – the Anglo-Italian Cup.

Some of you will never have heard of it, but it created quite a buzz at the time. It was a complicated competition which had been created the previous year, partly because Swindon Town – who had been in the Third Division at the time – had given the authorities a headache by winning the League Cup, as they were barred from playing in Europe due to their lowly status and facilities. Swindon went on to win the 1970 version of the Anglo-Italian Cup, although their final with Napoli had to be abandoned with them 3-0 up at the time due to serious crowd trouble. We'd heard a bit about the Italian fans, and some of the players, and their reputation for violence, so it didn't seem the wisest idea to give them some fresh English legs to kick.

There had been a lot of debate about whether it was worth repeating the exercise, but they went ahead with the Anglo-Italian Cup again in 1971, and Blackpool were lucky enough to be one of the six English teams invited to take part. We were in a group of four, along with Stoke, Verona and Roma, but would only play the two Italian teams in our group home and away. To reach the final, you not only had to win your group, but you also had to out-score the English teams in the other groups. Two points were awarded for a win, one for a draw, then an additional point for each goal you scored. I can guess what you're thinking and you're right – it was bloody hard to work out what the hell was happening, and the best thing to do was leave it to the mathematicians. All the emphasis was on attacking football, which meant some busy nights for me, but that suited me just fine. I wasn't going all the way to Italy to stand and watch the game. Nowadays, players are on a plane and on their holidays as soon as the season is over, complaining of fatigue and the need to recharge their batteries, but we had four games to play inside eight days – including two games in Italy – and no one grumbled. I was well up for it

– I had never even been on an aeroplane before. Budgie was about to get his wings!

We started off badly, and I saw a few goals fly past me – we drew 3-3 at home to Verona, but then lost 3-1 to Roma at Bloomfield Road. The Italians were generally quick, good on the ball and brutally physical when they needed to be. Somehow, though, we turned it round in our Italian double-header. We hit four past Verona then beat Roma 2-1 and to our amazement we were in the final thanks to the 10 goals we'd scored in the four games. The top-scoring Italian side were Bologna, so it was agreed we'd play the final in their stadium, the Stadio Renato Dall'Ara.

English football was the strongest in Europe at that time – Leeds had won the Fairs Cup and Chelsea had won the European Cup-Winners' Cup – so we were bidding for a treble. The Italians were desperate to salvage some pride, and we had been expecting it to all kick off if we got our noses in front. But it was a brilliant cup tie, played in the right spirit, and the Italians were nothing but sporting towards us on and off the pitch.

They took the lead, but our captain John Craven equalised to take it into extra time. Then in the first half of extra time Mickey Burns nabbed it for us. Our fitness was fantastic, and although the home fans were creating quite a racket, it only spurred us on. It was an amazing night.

Here's how the *Blackpool Gazette*'s reporter Patrick McEntee memorably saw the game from the press box...

The conquering heroes of Blackpool – every one of them who took part in the Anglo Italian League tournament but particularly the 13 who won the memorable final against Bologna – should get the freedom of the borough.

Being at this final was an unforgettable experience. Standing in the press box, I had a perfect view of Blackpool manager Mr Bob Stokoe's jig of delight along with the other Blackpool officials when the final whistle ended 120 minutes of gruelling action on a hot Italian night. The small but loyal band of Blackpool supporters, who had made their trip to Italy in charter flights, waved their union jacks and tangerine and white scarves high on the terraces. The disappointed Bologna fans, who did so much to restore one's faith in the sportsmanship of Italian soccer supporters, sportingly waved their red and black banners in tribute as the victorious Blackpool team did a lap of honour, skipper John Craven waving the 22-inch high gold trophy aloft. Another English team had triumphed against the odds in Europe and being British at that moment in the stadium was the supreme status symbol. Against the odds I said...and I mean every word. For the dice were loaded in favour of the Italians almost of necessity and Blackpool had to overcome the disadvantages that any visiting English team would have encountered. Remember, too, that they are a second division side, while Bologna finished fourth in the Italian first division. The biggest disadvantage was the heat. Despite a 5pm kick-off, the temperature in the sun-bleached stadium was in the high sixties, beautiful for the fans, murderous for British players. Blackpool had to fight its effect and the lung-bursting strain of the dry air, a combination that sent several of them tumbling down with cramp late in the game and in extra-time. On an occasion when most of the crowd were supporting the other team they also had to adjust their game to take account of the fact that the Austrian referee would allow little of the tackling we take as normal in the English game. And they disciplined themselves so superbly that they not only achieved this but gave Herr Schiller, whose decisions seemed to rather favour Bologna, no trouble at all. It's true Mickey Burns and Johnny Johnston were both booked but there was nothing aggressive about their offences. The game was impressively clean and sporting throughout, with hardly a bad foul in the entire 120 minutes. Both teams deserve a lot of credit for this. But briefly Blackpool won because they had in the end an apparently greater determination and will to win than the individually more skilful Italians. The way they picked up their weary legs to go into a half hour of extra-time, for men unused to such conditions, demanded character of the highest order. No praise is too high for the way these Blackpool players fought back from behind to win. They were all magnificent.

Blackpool: Burridge, Hatton, Bentley, Ainscow, Alcock, Suddaby, Burns, Green, Craven, Suddick, Hutchinson.

After we won the cup, we had a big civic reception in the town hall and the town square was all decked out in tangerine for us; it was like we had won the league – those scenes were absolutely unbelievable. When Blackpool won the play-offs under Ian Holloway in 2010 and returned to the Premier League – the first time they had been back there since I played – it very much reminded me of our celebrations nearly 30 years before. They are a great club Blackpool, with loyal supporters who make the team feel such an important part of the town, and I couldn't have been happier for them.

The year after we lifted the Anglo-Italian Cup, we were back to defend our crown. First up, we went to play Sampdoria in Genoa, another stunning city (most of them in Italy were, from what I remember) and using the experience we had picked up from the year before, we cruised to a 4-1 win. We knew how to play the Italians, and because the competition was all geared towards scoring goals, it didn't really suit their natural style of play. In Serie A, they would be used to games of cat-and-mouse where there might only be a maximum of one or two goals in the game. But in the Anglo-Italian Cup they had to open up if they wanted to progress in the competition and I think that definitely suited the English sides better. It certainly fitted in perfectly with Blackpool's style of play at that time, because the players we had were happy pressing forward. It was an interesting experiment, that's for sure, and I think the fans liked it too because they were pretty much guaranteed to be watching goals.

Before returning to England for our final two group games, we beat Lanerossi Vicenza 2-0. Back home, we again beat Sampdoria 2-0 – another clean sheet – but we saved the best till last, when we annihilated Vicenza 10-0 in a truly incredible match at Bloomfield Road on 10 June, 1972.

Mickey Burns and Alan Ainscow put us 2-0 up within two minutes and usually when that happens, the game settles into some kind of natural rhythm and the defence that has leaked the goals manages to tighten up a little. Not that night though! We simply kept raining goals down of them and they had no answers to our attacking power. Tommy Hutchison was marvellous in that match and he had a hand in just about every goal, while Alan Ainscow ended up getting a hat-trick. It got so bad for the Italians that their keeper Roberto Anzolin walked off the pitch when they 7-0 down, claiming he was injured and couldn't continue, but his replacement didn't fare much better and he was unable to do anything about stemming the flow of goals, letting in another three. I could have walked off the pitch at any stage myself for all I had to do on the night. I'd have been better getting myself a deckchair and a newspaper, because the Italians never looked like scoring. The upshot of the record-breaking 10-0 win was that we'd finished our four group games with a 100 per cent record, and with by far the best goal tally, so were in the final again.

This time however, against a very determined and well-organised Roma, there was no happy ending, and we were well beaten on the night in the Stadio Olimpico. Goals from Cappellini, Scaratti and Zigoni left us with no way back, and although Terry Alcock got us a last-minute consolation, that's all it was – consolation.

I really enjoyed the travelling and seeing new cities and a different culture first hand, and it gave me a taste for seeing more of Europe, which I'd enjoy again later in my career with Aston Villa and Hibs. I also enjoyed the bonuses we had been picking up hand over fist for our success in the tournament.

The first season, the club had rather generously offered to give us a tenner per man for every goal we scored, but because they had to fork out a fortune in bonuses, they had a rethink for 1972 and made it a fiver a goal. Maybe that's what spurred us on to hit 10 past Lanerossi. I wasn't complaining. Okay, it wasn't me who was scoring them, but I more than played my part with a lot of clean sheets and I was proud of my performances against some top-class players. It had made a refreshing change from the bread and butter matches of the English league and it was good to broaden my horizons.

CHAPTER 6

FAST CARS & FAST WOMEN

'I was going out drinking too much and pulling birds for fun. I was literally living life in the fast lane. Because I was hitting the clubs my mind was wandering.'

After our adventures in the Anglo-Italian Cup, I had a great big pile of bonus money burning a hole in my pocket. During my summer holiday, a couple of weeks before we were due to report back for pre-season training, I was on a train passing through Carlisle one day when I saw this fantastic car sitting gleaming in a garage forecourt. It felt like it was calling out to me for me to buy it. It was a Lotus Europa – the same kind of wheels George Best had at the time – and I thought to myself: 'I'm having that!'

The next chance I got I took the train back to Carlisle and swaggered into the garage, all cocky, and asked the salesman how much he was looking for. He looked me up and down and said: 'You couldn't afford it, son. It would cost you £20 to even take it for a test drive.' I peeled out some fivers and he reluctantly let me take it for a spin, with him sitting beside me in case I drove off into the sunset with it. He told me it would cost £1,300 to buy, but I could have it for £1,100 if I paid cash. 'No problem,' I said. 'Have it ready. I'll be back tomorrow.'

When I got there the next day, the salesman was waiting for me and after I'd shown him my bag full of readies he asked me to sit and wait for a moment while he sorted out the paperwork. He scuttled off, and after waiting for 10 minutes I saw two coppers arrive. They came straight up to me and asked me if I could pop into the office for a moment. 'Son, where did you get all this money?' one of them asked. 'I got it playing football,' I said.

When I said that, something clicked with the other policeman, and he asked: 'Are you John Burridge that used to play for Workington Reds?' I told him I was at Blackpool now, and that we'd just won the Anglo-Italian Cup and had a whole load of bonus money to spend. Thankfully they believed my story and that was the end of the little misunderstanding. The salesman said sorry for the inconvenience and then got his business head back on, desperately trying to salvage the deal. He explained to me that he had been suspicious that a young lad like me was in a position to buy such a flash car, and his first thought was that I'd been drug smuggling or robbing banks, because I was waving around a big bag of cash. That's why he had panicked and called the cops. He kept saying sorry and trying to butter me up, and although I was quite tempted to tell him to stick it up his arse, the bottom line was that I still wanted the Lotus. We did the deal, and off I drove – parking the car proudly outside my council house in Workington.

I loved that car, it was absolutely fantastic. I would take my mum for a spin to Keswick in it, or just head out at three in the morning, flying round the roads in the Lake District. Because it was the same car that George Best had, it gave me plenty of street cred, and it was a magnet for the girls who all wanted a shot in it. I'd found out what girls were for by this time, and had put my sexual encounter with the sofa behind me! Because

I had more money than I knew what to do with, I wasn't being at all careful and was giving it away to people and spending more than I should. I was going out drinking too much and pulling birds for fun. I was literally living life in the fast lane.

With the summer over, it was time to report for pre-season training, but each day when I headed to Bloomfield Road I would leave my Lotus hidden round the corner, because I didn't want to draw attention to myself and have the lads making a big deal of it. But one day, as I was sitting on the bus outside the ground with the rest of the team waiting to be taken to the training pitch, my car came whizzing round the corner and screeched to a halt in front of the bus. My first thought was that somebody had pinched it, but my heart sank when I saw the doors swing open and then Mickey Burns and Tommy Hutchison clamber out in their training kit. They climbed on to the bus grinning like Cheshire cats and waving the keys around. 'New car, Tommy?' Bob Stokoe asked Hutch, but when he said: 'No, this is Budgie's,' Stokoe was absolutely fuming, and he had every right to be angry. He must have been thinking to himself: 'I was buying this kid some clothes not so long ago, and here he is turning into a flash Harry.' I didn't have to wait long to find out what he thought about my new car. When I got back from training I was summoned down to the manager's office for a quiet word.

'Think you're in the big time now, do you?' he said, with the veins in his neck bulging. 'One minute, I'm having to buy you blazers and pants, now you're turning up in a fucking spaceship! You are meant to be a young footballer. I don't mind you buying yourself a car, but get something sensible, don't buy yourself a spaceship. Go away and have a think about what direction you want your football career to go.'

He was absolutely right, and I knew it was not the time and

45

place to be cheeky and to try and defend the way I had been behaving. It was time to take a long, hard look at myself. Because I had started drinking, going out with girls and hitting the clubs, my mind had started wandering – and it took Bob Stokoe to point it out to me. Money does affect you if you don't know how to handle it, especially when you are young and you have more money than sense. Saturday nights rather than Saturday afternoons had become the big thing for me, which was all wrong. I was right into Northern Soul music and dancing, and the Mecca nightclub – an absolute cavern of a place not far from Bloomfield Road – was one of the high spots for me to be seen on a Saturday night. The queues at the Mecca could be 300 yards long and three or four abreast to get in. But on a Saturday night, I would drive right up, throw my keys to one of the bouncers, and I'd stroll straight in. I was being distracted from my football with all the drinking, dancing and girls. I couldn't see it at the time but I had my priorities all wrong. I can see why Sir Alex Ferguson has made such a successful managerial career of keeping young players' feet planted firmly on the ground at Manchester United. With all the wining and dining I was doing, I wasn't playing anywhere near as well as I was capable of, my concentration levels were wavering, and I lost my place at Blackpool to George Wood, an excellent keeper who would go on to become a Scottish international.

I only had myself to blame. They had signed big George from Stirling Albion and he made an impact straight away. I realised I wasn't the big shot I thought I was and that I was definitely replaceable in Bob Stokoe's eyes. All of a sudden I found myself lost. I was in the wilderness. I had gone from being the hero, playing out of my skin, playing in the First Division and taking all the accolades, to just another fringe player in the Second Division. I took stock of the situation and decided that the first thing I needed to do was to dump the car. I took it back to the garage and they were quite happy to have it back at half the price. I swapped it for a Ford Capri, which was a little more professional and less flash than a Lotus Europa.

Len Graham, our trainer, did a lot of extra work with me, helping me work on crosses and I also became regimented doing my own intensive training. The local paper described my methods at the time, saying:

John's dedication is best illustrated by the commando-standard training schedule he sets himself:

Sunday: Six-mile fells walk in Lake District
Monday: Goalkeeping on the sands in the morning.
Weight-training afternoon and evening.
Tuesday: Mornings are for hard running; afternoons for shot saving.
Wednesday: Practice game in morning, weight-training after lunch.
Thursday: Sprint work. In evening, he coaches local team.
Friday: Agility work.

It wasn't only my car and my attitude that was changing; my life was about to change forever after a chance meeting with my future wife Janet. I was sitting on a wall outside my digs one day, feeling a bit devastated and down in the dumps because I wasn't in the limelight any more, when this girl walked by and caught my eye. She was younger than me – I was 19 at the time and she was 15 – but we started chatting away. She was telling me about her brother, how he played in a Subbuteo league, and after getting through a bit of small talk I arranged to see her again. She came round for me at the digs one night, and all the other lads were giving me stick, saying 'Budgie, your girlfriend is here to see you.' I was trying to protest that she wasn't my girlfriend, just a friend, but I didn't really care about all the ribbing I was getting – the truth was I was comfortable in her company and we just seemed to hit it off right away.

Her dad was the owner of Granthams Signs, a well known company in Blackpool, which had offices just over the road from the digs. I thought her family were quite posh – posh compared to where I had come from anyway – and they had money. They were all lovely people and I quickly became good friends with not only Janet but her family – her brother, sisters and her mum and dad.

I started to go round to their family home most nights. She wasn't one for drinking, even though she was too young anyway, so we would just spend quiet nights together, chatting away. If there was a match I was playing in nearby, she would come along and watch me. We were still just friends, rather than serious boyfriend/girlfriend, but after five or six months it blossomed into a proper romance. On a Saturday night, instead of going out for a drink like I had been doing before I met her, I would go for a walk with Janet, seeing the bright lights of Blackpool and having a natter. We got on like a house on fire and were just perfectly suited to one another. It was having a positive effect on my life – no more going out and behaving like an arsehole. I fell in love with her.

I got back into the first team and started to make the headlines again. Janet would try to be there to cheer me on every game. She would catch the supporters' bus down to away games. If we were playing down in London, the team coach wouldn't get back into Bloomfield Road until late at night, but she'd be sitting there in her duffel coat waiting for me. There were no mobile phones back then, so if we were running late she might have been sitting there for an hour or two. That's what I call devotion. Everything was fantastic. I moved out of the club digs and got my own place, and there was no doubt that Janet turned my life around – from going off the rails, she had got my career back on track.

It was all change at the top at Blackpool, too. Bob Stokoe, the man who had brought me to Bloomfield Road, left to take the Sunderland job. I wouldn't say he had been the nicest man in the world to play under; he was an old-fashioned, dour kind of manager, but he knew how to keep me on the straight and narrow and, looking back, I have a lot to be grateful for. With him, it was a case of 'Do it my way, or else' and he would put the frighteners up you all the time. But I won't take anything away from his achievements – he was a great manager, and his move to Sunderland proved to be an inspired one – he went on to win them the FA Cup, with another one of my future managers, Ian Porterfield, scoring the winning goal against Leeds United in 1973.

For that cup triumph, he was hailed as the Messiah of Sunderland. He came back to Bloomfield Road for a league game the next year with Sunderland and was getting a bit of stick from the Blackpool supporters who were calling him a traitor. I had been having a good game, but that was mainly his doing after he'd rattled my cage before the game. When we'd been heading out towards the tunnel before the match, the Sunderland players were walking past our dressing room door at the same time. Stokoe, in an effort to get the psychological upper hand, started slagging us off, pointing at me and a couple of the other Blackpool lads and saying: 'You're shit and you're shit.' That sparked me off a bit and I went out with a point to prove. Sunderland were awarded a penalty and I saved it. It was a tight game, and it was decided by a moment of genius. Mickey Walsh, who went on to become an Irish international, was only a youngster back then and had just broken into the team, but more or less straight from my penalty save he went down the other end, cut in from the right and hit a brilliant swerving shot with his left which flew past Jim Montgomery into the corner. It was such a great strike, it was voted goal of the season on *Match of the Day*.

Sunderland were a big scalp to take, the recent FA Cup winners, and after we had won 3-2 the Blackpool supporters were going crazy. Going up the tunnel after the game, I heard a familiar voice screaming and shouting at me. 'You moved! You moved before that penalty was taken.' It was Stokoe and he was raging at me. I was doing my best to just ignore him, but the old sod came right behind me and wellied me up the arse – a right hard toe-poke. I was furious, but when I turned round to ask him what the problem was, he kept at it, and started poking and pushing me in the chest. Stokoe had been a hard man as a player, and he was bellowing with rage. He'd lost the plot. When someone provokes me like that, I find it impossible to hold back. So, as he continued to shout in my face and push me, I felt I had no option but to defend myself and hit him with the old left hook/right cross combination. He went sprawling to the ground and his head hit the wall with a sickening crack. All hell broke loose in the tunnel. My team-mates were trying to pull me back and the Sunderland players were trying to retaliate, but in those days there were always fights in the tunnel. It was the norm. My team-mates were a bit shocked, too; after all I'd just decked our old boss. They managed to bring old Stokoe round and there was no real damage done. He didn't press charges because he knew he was in the wrong, but it was an unbelievable incident. He'd been good to me when he was manager, and I owed him a lot, but I have to say he was completely to blame after that game. He was too wound up about coming back to face his old club. He'd obviously copped for a lot of flak during the game from the Blackpool supporters, and tried to take it out on me. It was a bad move.

I was playing well and felt firmly back in the groove. I was keeping a lot of clean sheets and playing so well at the time that there were big stories going on in the papers, especially the *People* on a Sunday, that I was being lined up for a move to a First Division club.

Janet and I were saving to get married and had our eyes on a terraced house that was going to cost us £10,000. We were saving money and were looking for £4,000 to put down as a deposit. We had managed to save a couple of grand and her dad was going to put some in, but First Division wages would help my cause. There had been stories in the *People* that Manchester United were going to buy me, which was obviously very exciting to read. Tommy Docherty was in charge of United, who were about to be promoted again as Second Division champions after the unthinkable had happened the season before and they had been relegated. When we played them I had a really good game, and at the end of the match Tommy sought me out, patted me on the back, and said: 'See you at United in a week or two, son.' Nothing is ever certain in football, but to me that was all I needed to hear at the time – Manchester United wanted me and I would be going to Old Trafford before long. Alex Stepney was getting close to retiring and United were apparently on the lookout for a young goalkeeper. Because Blackpool was so close to

Manchester, people were putting two and two together and coming up with my name as the likely successor to Alex and that would have suited me nicely.

I was excited about the thought of signing for United and, after what Tommy had said to me, I thought it was only a matter of time before I got the call from Old Trafford. I heard nothing in the weeks since I'd spoken to Tommy Docherty, though, and I started the 1975/76 season still at Blackpool, with United going great guns back in the top flight. I had been at training one day in September and was getting changed when our trainer Len Graham came up to me and said: 'Budgie, the boss wants to see you.' This has to be good news, I thought to myself, because I'd been keeping my nose clean, playing really well and I knew a lot of big clubs were watching me, especially United. I had Manchester United on my mind as I headed into the office.

Harry Potts was the Blackpool manager by then and he said to me: 'Come in and sit down, son.' I knew what was coming next, or at least I thought I did, and it was all sticking closely to the script I had imagined as he continued: 'I've had to sell you, the club need the money. We've had an offer of £75,000 for you and we've got to take it.' So I said: 'Okay, where am I going – Manchester United?' But to my surprise, he told me I was being sold to Aston Villa. I asked him about United, but he explained that they'd only offered £50,000, and Villa had topped it by 25 grand. The player didn't have any choice in a situation like that – in those days you were sold to the highest bidder, so my dream of becoming a Manchester United player was dead in the water.

CHAPTER 7

HEROES AND VILLAINS

*'If you had to go to war and take only one man with
you, it would be Andy Gray.'*

It may have been a disappointment to learn that my move to
United wasn't going to happen for the sake of 25 grand, but
Villa were a massive club and the thought of moving to them still
appealed to me. They had bounced back from one of the darkest
times in their history, rising from the Third Division to the First,
and looked like a club that was going places. My move to Villa
Park unfolded at break-neck pace. I was told the Villa manager
Ron Saunders wanted me to head down to Birmingham to see
him straight away. So I got in my car, packed a bag and drove
down to the Midlands to see Ron. He said he wanted me to sign
a three-year deal, and if I agreed I'd be straight into the team on
the Saturday, just a couple of days later, against Birmingham in
the local derby at Villa Park.

The financial package they had put together was irresistible –
I would be on £500 a game, which was treble my wages from
Blackpool, and I'd be getting a £25,000 signing-on fee, which
was an awful lot of money and would pay for the house Janet

and I had set our hearts on. I didn't have much time to think about it, and although Saunders asked if I wanted to take a moment to go outside and think it over, I was on the spot and said yes.

Villa put me up in a hotel, and I rang Janet to tell her I'd signed. She was a bit worried about what going to happen to us, but I just said to her: 'Well, there's only one thing for it – we're going to get married.' It was as simple as that – not exactly a romantic setting, down on bended knee with violins playing in the background. I told her: 'I'm not driving home to Blackpool every weekend; I want you here with me.' Janet drove down to join me in Birmingham and she quickly set about the task of trawling estate agents for a house for us to set up home. She eventually found us somewhere near Lichfield, in a small village near the training ground. It cost us £16,000 and we paid cash for it. It was a beautiful house, five bedrooms with a big garden and we put it in both our names. I said I'd marry her on Valentine's Day that next year. Janet was my anchor, my guardian and I knew I'd have gone off the rails if she hadn't been there for me.

You can't ask for a more exciting start at a club than being pitched straight into the heat of a local derby. I was temporarily staying in the hotel. On the Friday night, I was trying to get my mind on the next day's game when there was a knock at the door. 'I'd like you to come down and meet Andy Gray; we've just signed him from Dundee United.' I had no idea at that stage what great mates we'd grow to become, and my first reaction was 'Who?' because I didn't know him from Adam – but I met him in the hotel reception and was told that he'd also be joining Villa, and although he wouldn't be cleared in time to play Birmingham, he'd be in the reckoning to face Middlesbrough at Ayresome Park the following week. Andy still came and watched the game, although he had to head straight back up to Scotland after to get his stuff.

Birmingham City had some great players like Trevor Francis and Peter Withe, but Ron Saunders didn't put too much emphasis on the team you'd be facing. He'd just turn to our big centre-half, Chris Nicholl, and say: 'You look after Withey, it won't be a problem to you.' There was a brilliant atmosphere, with almost 54,000 crammed into Villa Park, and despite trailing 1-0 at half-time we won it 2-1. Chico Hamilton equalised, then Brian Little scored the winner, and importantly for me I made some vital saves and had a cracking game on my debut. I became something of an instant hero to the Villa fans because we had won, and I played up to them with a bit of showmanship – a couple of handstands, and a bit of a gymnastics exhibition. It was the perfect start and I could see myself fitting in at Villa nicely.

Me and Andy swiftly became very good friends, but when we got to the training ground, I swear to God he was absolutely useless! I was thinking to myself, he's a cracking lad but Villa have got themselves a bit of a dud here. He was from a pretty tough home in Drumchapel in Glasgow and when he had gone home for the weekend he had obviously spent it catching up with his mates in the boozer. When he arrived back at the hotel in Birmingham, he was quickly looking for a drinking partner. Andy was a real livewire and he was a difficult man to say 'no' to when he was on a mission. He kept on at me: 'C'mon Budgie, come out for a pint.' So we went out, I had a couple of pints with him and then left him to it. He wasn't one for early nights and went on to a nightclub. I heard him rolling in later on, and it was clear he'd had a good time.

Since meeting Janet, I had become completely dedicated to my football again. I would have the odd pint now and then, but my days of wild binges were over. My routine was that from the Thursday, 48 hours before a game, I would stay in and start trying to prepare for the Saturday. But on the Thursday, I heard the hair-dryer going and there was Andy getting ready to hit the high-spots again. Janet came down to join me on the Friday, so I moved to a different room and left Andy to his own devices. On our way down to breakfast on the Saturday morning – after I'd done my little warm-up routine of stretches and a bit of running – I looked in on Andy's room. We had a big game, against Tottenham, and there he was snoring away, unbelievably worse for wear. So I left him in bed till about 12 o'clock. Ironically, Tottenham Hotspur had come to the same hotel for their pre-match meal, and they were all sitting there as I dragged a bleary-eyed Andy down to the dining room telling him something to eat would help put a lining on his stomach and straighten him up for the game. As Andy shambled into the dining room he saw Tottenham's big red-haired defender Willie Young, a Scottish international they had signed from Aberdeen. They knew each other and I think Willie was well known as a fiery character. As Andy walked past the Spurs lads, Willie couldn't resist a sly dig and shouted at him: 'Hey Andy, have you been out on the piss again?' Andy snapped back: 'Shut it, ya big freckled sheep!' The Scottish insults were flying back and forward at each other and there was a bit of a commotion.

I eventually managed to calm Andy down, because I think he was still a bit full of the jungle juice, and the two of us jumped into Janet's Volkswagen Beetle and headed down to Villa Park. The pre-match routine isn't like now, where you see players out on the pitch warming up, stretching and being put through training drills an hour before the game. Back in the mid-1970s you would just go out at five to three. Any warm-up routines were done in the dressing room. I was stretching off and banging the ball against the wall of the changing room from about 2.15, trying to get myself focused, but Andy had a different approach – by quarter to three there was still no sign of him. A search party was quickly raised, and after a hasty hunt for Villa's new star striker, just minutes before he was meant to make his home debut, they found him in the players' lounge watching the horse racing. He didn't even have his boots with him – he had left them in a plastic bag which he'd slung into the back of the Volkswagen and forgotten. It took Andy the best part of two minutes to get stripped while Janet went out to fish his boots out of the car. When Andy took them out the bag, they hadn't been washed for a week, there was still mud crusted on them and they were dry as a bone. Andy didn't bat an eyelid – cool as cucumber, he ran them under the tap, threw them on and then headed up the tunnel.

When the game started he struggled with the pace a little bit in the first few minutes, probably sweating the last traces of bevvy out of his system. But when we got a corner he took off like Superman, flying over the top of everyone to get on the end of it. He was only 5ft 11in and 11-and-a-half stone wet through, but he was unstoppable. He got his head on it and it was blocked on the line. It was a wet day, and he followed through, smacking straight into the post. It would have pole-axed most players, but Andy just got up, dusted himself down and got on with it. I was stood in the goals at the other end, thinking: 'God, what a header that was!' I was shouting up at him: 'Brilliant, keep it going.' They had Pat Jennings in goal and Andy went into him in a 50-50 and burst his face. At half-time, I turned to him and said: 'Brilliant, son, absolutely brilliant.' Now I knew what he was made of, because I wasn't sure at first. In the second half, he got his chance for a bit of retribution with Willie Young, and gave him an elbow right in the jaw. All the things that had been said about him at the hotel, he'd stored in the memory bank and waited for his chance for a bit of payback. I knew this lad could handle himself no problem! Then, just before the end of the game, another cross came in to the near post and he dived across to half-volley it with his head and score! I'd never seen anyone half-volley with their head. The game finished in a 1-1 draw, and Andy could be proud of his home debut. He wasn't hanging about after the game to be congratulated, though; he had his clothes on in no time and headed straight for the players' lounge for a few jars. Me and Janet were heading back to Blackpool immediately after the game for the weekend, but I heard they had to kick him out of there at half-eight because they were shutting it for the night. He just supped up and headed straight down the nightclub. He had been absolutely useless at training, so to witness what I had just seen on the football pitch was nothing short of amazing.

He was an instant hero at Villa, and the fans loved him. The saying that he 'would put his head where other people wouldn't put their foot' has become a bit of a cliché now, but the saying was invented for Andy Gray. He was utterly fearless, a brilliant footballer and a cracking lad, too. After that goal against Spurs, he was never off the scoresheet – forming a potent partnership up front with winger Ray Graydon, who had scored the goal that won Villa the 1975 League Cup – and Andy got us the winner when we beat Man United 2-1 at Villa Park.

I say to this day that Andy Gray is one of the best players I have ever played with. Kenny Sansom, later my team-mate at Crystal Palace, also has to be right up there, but Andy was something else. If I had to go to war and I could only take one man it would be him. He was an absolute warrior. He will always be like a brother to me, and such was his enthusiasm for football it was no surprise to see him carve out such a successful career as a pundit on Sky Sports. Obviously, that ended on a sour note, but I thought it was shocking the way he was treated. He said something off-air about a female assistant referee that he shouldn't have done, but he was treated like he'd committed some horrible crime. It's an absolute joke that he was sacked, but I'm sure Sky's loss will be some other broadcaster's gain. He could even come out here and reunite the old double act with me if he likes! I won't beat around the bush with all the politically-correct crap that brought him down, that's for sure! We've always looked after one another. He's had his share of divorce and heartache, but he has always been a fantastic person.

I was only 24 and was getting nearer my intended wedding day on 14 February, 1976. I thought it would be a great idea to get married on Valentine's Day, a touch of romance to impress Janet – but by a slice of bad luck it turned out that Valentine's Day that year fell on a Saturday and we had a game at Sheffield United. We had to get married on Sunday 15th instead, and although my last game as a single man ended with us losing 2-1, all the Villa team were out in force and in good spirits when we tied the knot the next day. All my old team-mates from Blackpool were there too, and it was a fantastic day.

The 1975/76 season maybe hadn't been one of the best on paper for Villa; we had finished only mid-table, but Ron Saunders was clever enough to play the long game and it was clear he had assembled a well-balanced team that was beginning to gel and mount a serious challenge for honours at home and in Europe in the seasons to come.

CHAPTER 8

LONG ROAD TO CUP GLORY

*'Brian Little scored in the last minute and to our
great relief we'd finally won the cup.'*

We started the 1976/77 campaign like a hurricane, opening
with a 4-0 win at home to West Ham, and recording some
big wins before Christmas – 5-2 against Ipswich, including a hat-
trick for Andy; 5-1 against Arsenal; 3-2 against Man U and 5-1
against Liverpool. We had sent out a clear message that not only
could we beat any team in the league on our day – we could tear
them apart.

We were also an incredibly fit team, which made me happy. I
absolutely thrive on hard training, and though I haven't found
many players willing to put in quite as much I do, Ron Saunders
made sure no one was allowed to shirk away from hard work on
the training ground. Most of our training was geared towards
running. Saunders didn't get too heavily involved in the tactical
side of football, and he was able to get successful results out of
the team mainly by signing skilful players and then training them
hard, to the point where they were fitter than any other club in
the league. He would have us running in ploughed fields and up

steep hills. There was plenty of moaning going on behind his back, because any footballer prefers to be training with a ball at his feet, but Saunders was a strict disciplinarian and wouldn't take any shit. He was ex-Army and his orders were to be followed. Training was unbelievably hard, but the results on the pitch justified his methods.

While we were showing some impressive form in the league, it was an incredible run in the League Cup that defined our season.

We saw off Manchester City (3-0), Norwich (2-1), Wrexham (5-1) and Millwall (2-1), all at home to set up a semi-final, over two legs, against Queens Park Rangers. There were lots of great players in that QPR team – Phil Parkes in goal, Frank McLintock, Dave Webb, Gerry Francis, Stan Bowles and Don Givens – and they would be a tough nut to crack, having already beaten us in the league that season.

The manager kept putting serious pressure on us that we had to win something or we would be regarded as failures. It was his job that was on the line too, but whereas some managers are good at shouldering the pressure themselves and shielding their players so they don't feel edgy, Saunders never hesitated to share the pressure around. We would later lose out in the quarter-finals of the FA Cup to Manchester United, and while we were riding high in the table the title looked out of our grasp, so he told us we simply had to win the League Cup to make sure we would qualify for Europe.

The first leg of the semi-final was on a frosty night at Loftus Road and it finished a 0-0 draw, which we were happy enough taking back to Villa Park. In the second leg, we were locked at 2-2 with about five minutes to go when QPR got a penalty. Don Givens, their star striker, ran up to take it, but I guessed right and stopped it. It was one of the most important saves of my career and I was cock-a-hoop. Aston Villa later built a fantastic stand at the tunnel end, and after that save I used to call it the John Burridge Stand, because if that penalty had gone in they would not have had the money to build it the following year. After extra time, we could still not be separated, so at the end of the game everyone was looking at each other, thinking: 'What happens now?' We were eventually told that the chairmen of the two clubs were going to reach an agreement on a neutral venue for a replay to be held. Our chairman was Doug Ellis at the time and he went to thrash it out with their chairman Jim Gregory. It was decided that a spin of the coin would settle the venue for a neutral ground – if it was tails, it would favour us, and the game would be played at Birmingham City's ground, if it was heads then it would favour QPR and the tie would be played in London at Highbury. Word filtered down to us that Deadly Doug had lost the toss and the replay would be settled at Highbury, but the popular story doing the rounds among the lads was that when the coin got thrown, it disappeared under a table with Jim Gregory scampering after it. When he re-emerged he was clutching the coin, shouting 'Heads'. Nobody had seen the coin, or so it was claimed. Doug would have been in an impossible position – he apparently asked for a re-throw, but Gregory wasn't having it and we were heading to Highbury.

As it turned out, it didn't matter where the game was played, because we blew them away. Brian Little was outstanding and finished off a hat-trick in the final few seconds, while I played my part and kept a clean sheet. We had cruised past them 3-0 and were heading for a League Cup final against Everton at Wembley.

The problem for me was that I was struggling to be fit for the biggest game of my life. Before the final, I had played in a 4-0 midweek win against Derby and taken a real crack on my kneecap. I had to sit out our match against Leicester the week before the final, and I was in doubt for my first game at Wembley. But while my knee was still agony, I thought to myself: 'I've got to play, it's a cup final for God's sake.' I kept the extent of the pain to myself, refused any further treatment, and declared myself fit to play. I wasn't nervous about the actual game at all, but I was more worried about my mum coming down safely on the train from Workington. When you were in a final at Wembley then, you were only given four complimentary tickets, but all my relations started to come out of the woodwork and were desperate to see me play my first game at Wembley. I had to get them for aunts and uncles, and by the time I had sorted them all out I had forked out for about 60 tickets myself! It was a far cry from a normal league game where you would get one or two people coming to see you. My mum was an old woman by then and I was worried sick about her making it all the way down from Workington because she didn't have too much experience of travelling. I needed something to relieve the tension and a practical joke in the team hotel was just the job. I was sharing a room with Andy, which was overlooking the car park. I had been looking out of the window when I noticed there was a big wedding party arriving. It didn't take much for me to get stupid ideas in my head back then, so I went to the bathroom and filled a bucket with water. Just as the bride and groom were coming I let fly with the bucket of water, tipping it over them. They were saturated. It was a horrible thing to do, I can see that now, but I was pissing myself laughing. I had been in two minds whether to do it, but my partner in crime, Andy, was egging me on: 'Do it, do it.' After I'd done the dirty deed, we went down in the lift to check out the damage. The two of us were sitting in the foyer sniggering away like schoolkids as they came in soaked and bewildered. I suppose we were still practically kids anyway. We were both working-class boys and I think the excitement of being in a big five-star hotel just got the better of us. The two of us were used to playing practical jokes on the rest of the lads in the dressing room, but this was maybe taking it a step too far. The next morning at breakfast, Ron Saunders came down and looked me straight in the eye as he asked: 'Who threw water over the bride and groom yesterday?'

'It wasn't me, boss. I've been preparing for the game, you know I have,' I lied, trying to put on an unconvincing choirboy face. Having now got that confession off my chest, I'd like to offer my belated apologies to Mr and Mrs Soaking-Wet – I hope your marriage has been a happy one since that day!

The final was played on 12 March, 1977 at Wembley and, as was the case for any cup final, it was a full house of 100,000. I remember meeting Princess Anne before the game. Chris Nicholl, our captain, was going along the line of players introducing us and when he came to me he said: 'This is John Burridge ma'am, the handsome one of the team.' She was married to Captain Mark Phillips at the time, so I gave her a cheeky look and said: 'Hello love, how are you? I'm not as handsome as your new husband, though, am I?' She burst out laughing and had a big smile on her face. All the lads were wondering what I'd said to her, fearing that I'd overstepped the mark with royalty and said something a bit too risqué that was going to get the club into trouble. Everyone else had been very straight-laced, keeping their responses to the standard 'Pleased to meet you ma'am.' I bet you she hadn't been counting on being confronted by a jackass like me!

It was a strange game, and almost entirely forgettable to be honest, and it finished in a drab 0-0 draw. It was a strange feeling at full-time because everything had been planned for us winning that cup, and here we were heading home empty-handed and with a replay to prepare for at Hillsborough four days later. It's a far better set-up today, finishing finals on the day with extra-time and penalties if they're needed.

When we got back to the hotel, the atmosphere was as dead as a doornail because nothing had happened one way or the other, and everyone's minds had already turned to the replay. I was in bed watching the highlights of the final on *Match of the Day* by 10.30 and any cup winner's party would have to wait.

We returned to Birmingham on the Sunday, before we then headed to Sheffield on the Monday. For the replay on the Wednesday it was a full house again, 55,000 this time, and we went one-up when Roger Kenyon scored an own goal. It was a crap game, but it looked like we'd done enough until Bob Latchford equalised in the last minute to take it to a second replay.

The third game was to be played at Old Trafford, almost a month later. In a cup final you should be turning up expecting to win or lose, so it was strange when there was still nothing decided. A lot of tension was building up, with Ron Saunders so desperate to get us into Europe. He was uptight for every game leading up to the final, because it was hanging over us and was a bit unsettling.

We were a bit weakened for the final too – Andy and John Gidman were out of the team injured. The first two matches against Everton had been pretty awful but the third clash was an absolute classic. There were 55,000 inside Old Trafford, and although a couple of our key men were missing I think our fans could still sense it was going to be our night. I remember making a good stop from a Latchford header, but he still put them in front. Chris Nicholl hit an absolute corker from 35 yards to equalise in the second half, and when Brian Little scored a couple of minutes later I was thinking to myself that's got to be it all over. But again – with one Villa hand seemingly on the trophy – Everton forced it into extra-time when Mike Lyons scored after a goalmouth scramble. It didn't look like we would have a winner at the end of that 30 minutes either, but Brian scored in the last minute and to our great relief we'd finally won the cup.

As I went up the steps to get my medal, I gave a wink to my new royal pal Princess Anne, and then after a lap of honour on the Old Trafford pitch the jubilant Villa team headed for a well-earned knees-up. After all, that champagne had been on ice for a month!

CHAPTER 9
THE DOUR RON RON

*'Saunders was putting so much pressure on me.
I would have known how to handle it if I had
been older.'*

When I was at Blackpool the expectations weren't unbearably high, but at Aston Villa we were constantly under pressure to win something. It would have been exactly the same at Liverpool, Manchester United, Rangers or Celtic – it's a good thing to have at a club when the fans demand success. But at Villa, in those days, it seemed a big ask. It had been great winning the League Cup, and all credit to Ron Saunders for the job he was doing, but I started to get irritated with the way he was treating me. He was always putting me down and that started to affect my confidence. I was in a very strong team at Aston Villa and we had players who were capable of beating anyone in that league. But I had been bought for almost a hundred grand and was expected to perform like a veteran – something I was 10 years short of. I had a lot of experience for my age maybe, but I was a long way short of having the type of life experience needed to cope with the demands of the job. The pressure was really getting to me. I started to get irritable and was arguing with my wife when I got home. I was finding it harder and harder to put my football problems to one side, and it was all I thought about.

Saunders was putting so much pressure on me. I would have known how to handle that if I had been a bit older. But when you are in your early 20s, in goalkeeping terms you're still a bit of a baby. I needed an arm round my shoulder sometimes instead of being continually criticised. I was always a fighter though, whatever crap was chucked at me, and I kept my place in the team throughout the League Cup-winning season because of my battling qualities.

Saunders had been an excellent striker for Portsmouth in his day and we would do a lot of crossing and volleying on the training ground, which he liked to join in. He could still hit the ball well and was a good header of the ball too and sometimes he and Andy would work as a pair, one on the near post and one on the back post. But whenever he scored a good goal, maybe one he'd hit it on the volley from seven or eight yards, he would be right over and in my face shouting 'You should have saved that!' It was getting to me. If I'd been older, I would have just laughed it off. But I had a notoriously short fuse and I ended up going for him...going for the MANAGER! Next ball that came over, I battered into him, but he still had the last laugh – the ball ran through for Andy to score at the back post. It was confrontations like that that did me no favours at all, and if a player clashes with a manager, the odds are stacked against the player ever winning.

After a couple of years of him sniping it was getting to me – I was getting increasingly unhappy and angry. I thought to myself 'I need to get away from this guy.' At first, Villa wouldn't contemplate letting me go because I was playing well. I would have loved to have gone on and had a long and happy spell at Villa, because they were an absolutely fantastic club, with great players – Brian Little, Dennis Mortimer, Alex Cropley, Andy Gray, I could go right through that team. But it didn't really matter who my team-mates were, I found Ron Saunders unapproachable and difficult to get on with – he was a very serious, dour person – and if you're unhappy then there isn't much point hanging around.

I was flattered that he had signed me in the first place, but there was no way we were ever going to get on and our contrasting personalities (I had one, he didn't) clashed over and over again. To give you an example, we went away to Greece for an end of season break, just a bit of a piss up for the lads and a bit of team bonding. We were all sitting round the pool, having a beer and chatting, when this poser in his tight Speedos at the other end of the pool started doing fancy flips off the diving board into the pool – he was trying everything to impress the girls who were sunbathing by the side of the pool. He really fancied himself and was getting on all the lads' nerves, strutting like a peacock and making a nuisance of himself with all his splashing about. They were egging me on to shut him up and put him in his place. I'd had a couple of beers, which I still wasn't able to handle very well, so without any further ado I flipped myself onto my hands and started walking round the pool upside down. Ron Saunders was watching me like a hawk as I walked on my hands past the poser, shuffled on to the diving board then jumped into the pool, arse over tit. 'How about THAT then, girls!' I shouted when I surfaced. The lads were hooting with laughter as the poser sloped away, his macho pride dented by the clown. It was just a bit of light-hearted fun, but Saunders didn't like that kind of thing. I had only done it for a bit of team spirit, but any showmanship seemed to make Ron bristle. Instead of turning a blind eye or trying to see the funny side, he just gave me that cold, steely look and told me to grow up.

Another time I really got under his skin was when we were coming back from a European game and were making our descent into Birmingham airport. Ron Saunders was the worst flyer you have ever seen in your life – he was frightened to death. He used to down about six tranquilliser tablets and a bottle of whisky before he'd even set foot on a plane. He used to insist on taking the middle seat, with the trainer Roy McLaren beside him, and the club doctor on the other side. Unfortunately for him on that occasion, it was the 'bad boys' of Aston Villa that were sitting directly behind him. I had Andy on my left and John Gidman on my right, and the temptation to wind him up was too great for me to resist. Earlier in the journey, I had been chirping away behind him. As we were flying over a mountain range, I was loudly saying to Andy and John that if the weather turned bad, the plane might go down. I was taking great satisfaction from watching Ron squirming uneasily in his seat in front of me. It was a bit cruel, but I was fed up with all the shouting and screaming from him on the football field and training ground, so it was my little way of getting him back.

As we approached the runway at Birmingham, just a matter of feet from the ground – the bit where everyone gets a little bit nervous and takes a deep breath – I decided it was time to go in for the kill and sock it to him. I got hold of my sick bag from the back of his seat, blew it up as far as it would go, then made a knot in the end. I showed it to Andy and John Gidman, and, just as they were trying to say: 'No Budgie, don't do it...', I leant over him with my bag all pumped up like a crisp packet and smashed it right behind his ear. It went BANG and Saunders went sliding down to the floor screaming. Roy

McLaren turned round and punched me right in the face. The doctor turned round and said: 'You idiot, you could have given him a heart attack!' I was full of adrenaline and started screaming back: 'I wish I *had* given him one!' The players were in uproar, everyone was pissing themselves, and it was pandemonium as we came to a standstill on the runway. He never said a word to me when we got back to the airport terminal; he looked like he'd seen a ghost. I lost my place in the team for that stunt, he dropped me immediately.

After our League Cup-winning run and our qualification for Europe I had plenty of money tucked away in the bank – Villa were a generous club and were quick to reward success. Life may have been good financially, but I was so young and the pressure from Saunders was mounting. I could see my days at Villa were numbered because I was becoming very unhappy and the spring had gone from my step. I was being well paid and we had a great team but I just could not take the pressure. It was too much for a lad of my age. If I had been playing under a manager who could have handled me properly and nursed me through the bad times a bit I would have stayed, but Saunders was a real bully boy.

I've never played for Alex Ferguson, and I know he has mellowed to an extent with age, but over the years he has struck me as being in a similar mould to Saunders. You can bully a midfield player or bully a defender or a forward, but you can't bully a goalkeeper. A goalkeeper needs to be full of confidence at all times. If a manager is slagging you off, then your confidence nosedives. If he's right up in your face giving you the hair-dryer treatment – and most of them were a bit like that in those days – it is the wrong thing to do when dealing with a young keeper. A midfielder can make a misplaced pass or a striker can miss an open goal but for a goalkeeper there is no hiding place. You don't get away with it. I don't care what anyone says, the most important position on the football field is the goalkeeper. You always get remembered for your mistakes, and Saunders made damn sure I remembered all of mine. I was on the verge of a nervous breakdown. I had it out with him in his office one day and he called me a 'pussy' – maybe I was, but to play in goal for a club like Aston Villa at such a tender age, you had to be a certain type of person, mentally unbreakable. When I later went to Crystal Palace I always had Terry Venables telling me how good I was and that would fill me with confidence and I would take that on to the pitch. But man management wasn't Saunders' strong point. The records show he is a Villa legend, and one hell of a manager in terms of success, but I never took to the man. After my own experiences, particularly with Saunders, I always put goalkeepers at ease when I coach them now, try and tell them they are the best even if they are not. If you hammer them it's the worst anyone can feel because I've been through it myself.

Even now when goalkeepers are blamed for goals, I always try to take the goalkeeper's side. Even though deep inside my heart I know they are to blame for the goal, I will always stick up for them.

It was clear that my relationship with Saunders had deteriorated to the point that I knew I had no future at Villa Park, so I slapped in a transfer request which was accepted in an instant by the manager. To speed up my departure, he signed a new goalkeeper not just to challenge me for the gloves, but to directly replace me. I was out on the training ground one morning and I saw the manager striding towards us with another goalkeeper by his side. I recognised him straight away – I'd seen him before playing for Manchester United a few years before. It was Jimmy Rimmer, who he had bought at a knock-down price from Arsenal reserves. He was a top-class keeper, but Pat Jennings had been keeping him out of the first team and he was too good to be sitting in the reserves. Saunders pulled us all together and introduced him to the team. We all shook his hand and wished him all the best, but while I was putting a brave face on it, inside I felt a little bit pissed off. Even though I had asked for a transfer and I knew I'd soon be heading to another club, I couldn't help feeling a bit jealous.

Jimmy was a good guy and a very good keeper, and I had nothing against him personally, but my pride was bruised and I was feeling like yesterday's man and I felt the need to lash out a bit. In one session, we were practising free kicks and corners, and Saunders ordered me to get out of the goal and told Jimmy to go in. It was a fair enough call, as he needed to work the man who would be playing on Saturday, but he made me feel so insignificant that I was raging inside. The mistake he made, though, was putting me with the forwards for the training drill. I put on a bib and joined the attackers, and just before it was my turn to try to get on the end of a cross, Andy Gray came up behind me and said under his breath: 'Budgie, this is a golden opportunity for you. Dinnae hold back, fuckin' whack him.' That was all the encouragement I needed, and Andy the mischief-maker must have known that. So when ball got fired over, a low near-post ball, I came flying in on Jimmy and kneed him, sending him onto his arse. Why I did it I'll never know. As I headed back to join the rest of the forwards at the halfway line, they were all laughing their heads off, especially Andy who had been the instigator. But he wasn't finished, and neither was I. 'Budgie, that was nothing, surely you can do better than that?' said Andy. So I tried the same again, except this time, Jimmy saw it coming and managed to ride the challenge a bit better. But Saunders wasn't going to let me crock his new keeper and hollered at me: 'That's enough!' He took the bib off me and, not to put too fine a point on it, told me to 'get the fuck off the training ground.' I didn't care, but I still wouldn't give in to him, I was way too stubborn just to head back to the changing rooms like a chided schoolboy. Instead, I went and stood behind the goals, mooching about for the rest of the session in a huff.

I was sent to play for the reserves and I hated it. I had been used to playing First Division football, and all of a sudden I found myself at places like Port Vale – playing in front of three men and a dog. I thought 'Shit, what's going on here?' I hadn't a clue how to handle the situation. I swallowed my pride one day and went to see Saunders. 'I'm finding it hard to play reserve team football,' I told him. 'Until a club comes in for me, can I go out on loan somewhere?' Give him his due, he was accommodating and said he would try his best and see what he could do for me. He was true to his word, and it was put in the papers that I was available for loan. About a week later, Southend United came in for me. I think it was fated that I would play for them one day, because a funny thing had happened to me a few years before when I was at Workington – I'd had a strange dream about Southend. Before I had even set foot in Southend, I'd dreamt all about their ground, exactly how it looked, and even the correct score before we played them – it would be Southend 1, Workington 1. When I went there on the bus with Workington, I turned to the manager Brian Doyle and said: 'I've been here before – I've dreamt about it.' I think Brian just shrugged it off as me being a bit eccentric as usual, but I swear everything was exactly the way imagined it – right down to the score, 1-1! So there was always something lingering in the back of my mind about Southend, and it was an easy choice to go out on loan to them. Without hesitation I said I would rather be playing for Southend than Aston Villa reserves. Okay, it was Fourth Division, but their manager Dave Smith was a cracking bloke and everyone at the club made me feel so welcome. Janet and I stayed in a nice boarding house right on the sea front, which reminded us of Blackpool, and I stayed on the same salary I was on at Villa.

Dave's enthusiasm for the game was infectious and he knew his football too. The club were going places under him, and it may have been the Fourth Division but they had to start somewhere. I played six games and we won them all. We beat Bournemouth, Scunthorpe, Halifax and Southport at home, and beat Crewe and York away. I enjoyed the games, and with no disrespect to the players in the Fourth Division, found it easier to play against them after playing in the First Division. They weren't as sharp or quick to react, and as a goalkeeper I found I was able to read the game far, far easier at that level and although I let in one or two, my form held up very well.

Dave Smith was on at me to stay, telling me of his masterplan to bring Southend up the divisions, but I was always honest with him. I saw my future in the First Division, albeit not with Villa, or at least with a team in the Second Division that had realistic prospects of promotion. I was really enjoying my spell at Southend, and the sea air reinvigorated me. After being down in the dumps at Villa, I was back to my happy-go-lucky ways, and was enjoying life and football again. Southend was less than an hour's drive to London and I would hook up with a good friend I had there called Barry Silkman, who played for Crystal Palace. As fate would have it, he would be the key figure in finding me a permanent new club after Villa.

I had met Silky on holiday in Morocco and we had kept in

touch. While I was at Southend, I would head across to London and together with the wives we would go to the pictures and have meals. One night, Silky – who has become a successful football agent now – dropped into the conversation that Palace might be looking for a keeper, and that he'd see what the lie of the land was. The wheels for a move to Palace were in motion.

Southend usually played on a Friday night to help swell their crowds, because a lot of local folk used to go off and watch one of the London teams on a Saturday. So I took advantage of one free Saturday and I went along to watch a Palace game. I liked the feel of Selhurst Park the moment I set foot inside. They were a huge club, and it took me a bit by surprise. The biggest draw though was their young up-and-coming manager Terry Venables. He was a breath of fresh air after Ron Saunders' bully boy tactics. An official approach was made to Villa, and though I felt bad about disappointing Dave Smith at Southend, it was no contest.

My short roller-coaster ride at Villa was at an end, but I couldn't resist one naughty parting shot at Saunders and his coaching team.

We all had club cars in those days. I had an Alfa Romeo, a neat little sporty number, and I was told it would be going to Roy McLaren, our trainer. It was a lovely car and I had kept it immaculate, but I didn't like the way I was told gruffly to return it pronto – or else – so I thought I would leave them a little surprise. I was due to take the car back on a Monday morning, but before dropping it off at the stadium I took a detour to the local farm near my house, had a word with my farmer pal, chucked 10 chickens inside the car and let them do their worst! Can you imagine all the chicken shit 10 of them could make in an enclosed space? It wasn't a pretty sight...or smell.

I put a towel down on the driving seat to cover up the mess my feathered friends had made, and took it down to Villa and handed back the keys. Roy McLaren went striding outside thinking he was about to get himself a beautiful car, but when he looked inside all he saw was chicken shit and feathers. The look on his face was perfect – he was absolutely devastated. I was pissing myself laughing. I went inside and told all the lads and they came out to see it. It was Budgie 1, Authority Figures 0!

So, it was farewell to Villa, and when they went on to conquer Europe not long after I left, with Jimmy Rimmer an absolute hero for them in goal, it was a strange feeling. Did I have any regrets and a sense of what might have been? Hell yes! I would have loved to have stuck around in that team that won the European Cup two years later, but I did the right thing at the time.

It worked out well for Villa too because they bought the perfect replacement for me. They were wise enough to go for someone like Jimmy Rimmer, who was a good bit older than me and had experience that money can't buy after his time at Manchester United and Arsenal. To be brutally honest, and I like to think I'm man enough to admit it, if I had stayed and not asked for a transfer I don't think Aston Villa would have won the European Cup with me in goal. It's a long and arduous road to win a European trophy, there's an awful lot of mental pressure involved, and the way I was at that time I'm not sure I could have handled it. Jimmy did a great job of it, but he had the experience I was lacking, and dealt with whatever was thrown his way. The following year, my new club Crystal Palace drew Villa in the League Cup. It was a 0-0 draw at Selhurst Park and we went back to Villa for the replay. When you've left a club you are always a bit wary because sometimes it can be a bit of a grudge game, but in the replay the Villa fans were brilliant towards me. I played an absolute stormer, and we battled to a 1-1 draw. They were even more charitable towards me in the second replay, because they beat us 3-0!

CHAPTER 10

CLOWN PRINCE OF THE PALACE

'Terry Venables taught me more in six months than anyone else had taught me in 16 years.'

I t's safe to say that Terry Venables created a very favourable impression on me from the first time we met. We concluded the signing talks in the Royal Lancaster Hotel, next to Hyde Park, and I warmed to his personality immediately. There was something about his Cockney accent that had me mesmerised. He knew how to make me feel at ease, laughing all the time but at the same time passionate and deadly serious about his football.

Around the same time as my Palace move, Janet and I had some good news – she was pregnant. It was a hurly-burly time for us in our lives. I had expected Selhurst Park to be small compared to Villa Park, but it was a huge cavern of a ground. Before I signed on the dotted line I was invited down to watch a youth team match against Arsenal. Palace's youngsters were sensational and won 3-0. I couldn't believe it when I turned up at training and found that most of the kids I'd been watching in the youth game were also my new first-team team-mates. To emphasise what a good crop of youngsters they had coming through, they won the FA Youth Cup in 1977 and 1978, beating my old club Villa in the second final.

It was such a young side, but the spirit was fantastic. I was practically the old man of the team at 24, along with the centre-half Jim Cannon and Stevie Kember. There was so much talent in the team: Kenny Sansom, the left-back, was only 17 and absolutely magnificent; then there was Paul Hinshelwood at right-back; Vince Hilaire on the right wing; Jerry Murphy and Peter Nicholas the Irish and Welsh internationals in midfield; and Ian Walsh, another Wales cap, up front.

I felt at home right away. I loved going in to training, having a bacon sandwich and a laugh with the lads beforehand – Crystal Palace was just one big happy family. I was well looked after. Terry always did everything with a smile on his face. His coaching was incredible. Terry Venables taught me more in six months than anyone else had taught me in 16 years. He knew how to dismantle a team, make it better, then put it back together again. No more running on ploughed fields, like I had done at Villa under Ron Saunders; this was cutting-edge training. Terry was way ahead of his time. He recognised that a footballer will only run 70 yards at one time. Most of the time was spent on technical play – how to defend, when to defend, how to think outside the box, how to make runs from midfield. I really enjoyed the way Terry trained me and the goalkeepers, and how he involved the team in his way of thinking. I think a lot of that team benefited from how Terry involved them that way. At a lot of clubs, you just go out and do what you're told and you're none the wiser, but Terry would explain his reasoning behind a certain training drill or exercise, and I think all of us broadened our football knowledge working under him.

I had arrived towards the end of the 1977/78, initially on a loan agreement before a permanent contract could be signed, and we finished mid-table, but already full of hope and optimism for the following season, 1978/79. After a good pre-season, we started like a steam train, and the crowds were flocking in to see us. We got 30,000 for a 1-1 draw at home to West Ham, but our real arch-rivals at that time were Brighton and Hove Albion, and Selhurst Park was absolutely jammed for that one, there was a huge crowd in. It was starting to dawn on me that this could be a massive club if managed properly – and they certainly had the right manager sitting in the dugout.

The Brighton match would normally have been the type of game to make even a seasoned pro a little bit nervous, but these kids were oblivious to pressure and were totally fearless. Before the game, we were all sitting around in the players' lounge, with Kenny Sansom, who was a bit of a betting man, acting as the bookie and taking bets for the lads. It was such a relaxed atmosphere. They were all just sitting around eating Mars bars an hour before one of the biggest games of the season. Terry would come and round up the team about 2.15, and they would then just slip effortlessly into match mode. The dressing room was like a kids' playroom sometimes. For Palace fans at that time, beating Brighton meant everything, and we didn't let them down – winning 3-1 thanks to a double from Vince Hilaire and one from Dave Swindlehurst. If the atmosphere had been good in the dressing room beforehand, it was absolutely jumping when we came in at the end of 90 minutes.

I started to really enjoy myself. Crowds at Selhurst Park kept getting bigger, and we were winning games for fun and keeping clean sheets along the way. Our brand of football was brilliant. Defensively we were tight, we were creative in the middle, and we had the killer instinct up front – all the ingredients of a successful, well-balanced side. Kenny Sansom probably best typified what a confident, swashbuckling team we were. I remember the dying seconds of one game, where I picked the ball up and was getting ready to hoof it upfield to waste some seconds and close out the game. Kenny was having none of it, and was screaming at me to give the ball to him wide on the left. When I looked over and saw he had a marker lurking 10 yards away from him, I told him to get up to the halfway line. I ignored his pleas and punted the ball up the middle of the park, but their centre-half won it and it came right back to me. Again, there was Kenny – bellowing at me like he had before to give him the ball. Reluctantly, this time I did. He controlled the ball in the left-back position, played a one-two with Jerry Murphy, carried it another 30 yards, played another one-two with Dave Swindlehurst, then swung a lovely ball in for Ian Walsh to stick in the back of the net. Kenny wasn't done though – he ran the length of the pitch, heading straight for me, and shouted: 'THAT'S why you should give me the fucking ball!' I just shrugged my shoulders and said 'Hey, okay son. If you can do that – you can have the ball anytime!'

It didn't surprise me in the slightest that Kenny went on to become such a star for Arsenal and England. He just oozed confidence and was built like a brick shithouse. He was tiny, but strong and barrel-chested, and his control, timing and skill were remarkable for a full-back. I hardly ever kicked a ball out from hand after that at Crystal Palace. I would throw it out most of the time to let Kenny and the others do their thing. Terry preferred it that way anyway – building from the back – and he would always encourage slick, passing football.

There was so much enthusiasm coursing through the side and the fans fed off it. It was November before we lost our first game in the Second Division. We only lost four games out of 42 league matches all season. We lost to Fulham at home 1-0,

Bristol Rovers, Burnley and Sheffield United. It was cast-iron promotion form. The football side of my move was going absolutely brilliant, while off the pitch it was working out well too. When we first arrived at Palace, it had all been a bit of a rush trying to find somewhere to stay, so the club had found us a flat in Brixton. It was a bit of a scary street and the smell of weed was overpowering in our stairwell, but I actually liked the cosmopolitan feel of the place. I always embraced new places and new cultures, probably because I came from a mining village and realised that the rest of the world could teach me a lot. But after moving out of our Brixton billet, Janet and I had settled into a lovely townhouse in Surrey and had adapted well to the good life in London. We would go out in the West End, to the pictures or to have a bite to eat. I may have had a few misgivings about London when I was living in the north, but I really enjoyed it there. There were so many things to do to take your mind off football and it felt a privilege to be living there and playing for such a great manager and great club, even if they were Second Division.

But sometimes, just as you think life is pretty much perfect, it has a habit of kicking you right in the teeth, and our world took a serious jolt when Janet ran into trouble with the baby. I got a call when I was at the training ground saying I had to get home right away as Janet was in terrible pain. I drove there in five minutes flat and was by her side as we rushed to the hospital, gripped with fear. Janet had only been seven months pregnant, and was about to go into premature labour. The doctors warned me that there may be something wrong with the baby. I'm not a deeply religious man by any means, but I got right down on my knees and prayed that Janet and the baby would be okay. The hospital staff did all they possibly could, but we lost our first baby. It was a little boy, and he only weighed 2lbs. He was alive for 20 minutes, but we had lost our first child. We hadn't named him, but he will always be in our thoughts. I still went in to training the next day, in a complete daze, and when I returned to the hospital to see Janet, she was absolutely devastated with our loss. It was one of the most horrible days of our lives. Her mum and dad came down from Blackpool to be with her, and I tried to take my mind off it the only way I could – training hard and playing football. It never put me off my game, and I shut it away at the back of my mind. Thankfully, with time Janet recovered, and happily we would later go on to have a family. Our son Thomas arrived in September 1979 and our daughter Katie was born in May 1982.

Palace's winning run showed no sign of slowing down, and we were sitting proudly on top of the league. But another problem was just round the corner for me – this one physical. We were playing Bristol Rovers at home on Boxing Day at Selhurst Park. I remember a ball being played into the box and as I went in to make a challenge, their striker Bruce Bannister collided with me and knocked my left shoulder out. It was an absolute mess – I had torn ligaments and dislocated it. To rub salt into the wounds, he scored and we lost the game 1-0, only our second League defeat of the season.

As soon as I came off the field I knew my shoulder was badly injured and that there would be no quick fix. A few days later we were due to play Leyton Orient at home. I was really struggling to move my shoulder, but Terry was saying: 'Budgie, we need you, you've got to play.' So from Boxing Day onwards that season, I was basically playing with only one good shoulder. I used to see the club doctor and get cortisone injections before each game to help numb the pain. You are only really meant to get one, but sometimes I would be getting three before the game and three at half-time just to get me through the 90 minutes. For the rest of the week, in between matches, I wouldn't be able to train properly. I would just do lots of running and some stomach exercises to keep up my basic fitness. I found that incredibly frustrating because I used to love diving about in the mud all week and doing all my weight training, but because of the state my shoulder was in, anything too strenuous was impossible. I was suffering a bit, but I had a bit of good news at home to help me grit my teeth and get through it – Janet was pregnant again, with Thomas on the way.

I may have been patched up for every game, but I was still playing well. The buzz created by my team-mates was just as good as any injection. The whole place had a feelgood factor, and we had a steely determination to not only win promotion to the First Division but to win the championship and go up in style. Sore shoulder or not, I very much wanted to play and be part of that. A lot of teams would try to shut up shop against us, and although one or two of them succeeded, we never panicked. Even the odd game where we did not play particularly well, Terry was crafty enough and tactically shrewd enough to ensure we took something out of the match. If we kept it tight at the back and had a bad day in front of goal, then a 0-0 draw and a point would be no disaster as they were all adding up to consolidate our place at the top of the table.

It was a thrilling title race, probably one of the most open and exciting there has ever been in English football, and I think everyone sensed that it was going to go right down to the wire. There were five very good teams in the Second Division, all worthy of making the step up – West Ham, Sunderland, Stoke, us and our big rivals Brighton. We'd wobbled a bit in April, drawing with Oldham and Cambridge and losing up at Newcastle. With six games to go, we were sitting fourth – our lowest league position since August. With just a couple of points separating the big five, we felt we needed to win all six matches to secure the title, and maybe four or five to clinch one of the three promotion spots. First up, we won 1-0 at Bristol Rovers, then we did the same at home to Charlton. The following week, we were losing 1-0 at Leicester but fought back to salvage a point, although that kept us in fourth and just outside the promotion spots. Some wrote off our title chances at that some stage, but it was still incredibly tight at the top, and we felt if we could win our last three games anything was possible. We set about the challenge with relish – we beat Notts County, who were sixth, 2-0, then pipped Orient 1-0 in a tense game to keep our dream alive. The weird thing about that match was that it should have been our last game of the season – but we'd had a match with Burnley postponed during the winter, so while everyone else had played their 42 games, we had one still to play. We would face Burnley the following Friday in a win or bust game at Selhurst Park. West Ham had faded out of the equation, but on the same day that we'd won at Orient, our other three remaining promotion rivals Brighton, Stoke and Sunderland had all won too, so we were still frustratingly in fourth spot – yet a tantalising one win away from snatching the league at the death.

The top of the table before that final nail-biting game read:

	Pld	W	D	L	F	A	PTS	GD
1 Brighton	42	23	10	9	72	39	56	+33
2 Stoke	42	20	16	6	58	31	56	+27
3 Sunderland	42	22	11	9	70	46	55	+24
4 Crystal Palace	41	18	19	4	49	24	55	+25
5 West Ham	42	18	14	10	68	39	50	+31

It was an unbelievable scenario. If we lost, we would stay fourth and miss out on promotion. If we drew, we would sneak into third place. If we won, and took the two points (as it was for a win back then) we would be champions at the expense of our biggest rivals that season – Brighton. A draw or a win for us would deny Sunderland promotion and, even more importantly to the Palace fans, snatch the title away from Brighton. Burnley were comfortably mid-table, but were aware that the rest of the league would be rooting for them to spoil our party, and there was no way on earth they were going to do us any favours and take it easy. Plus, they had been the first team to beat us in the league that season, back in November, so that added to the jitters too because we knew they were an awkward and well-organised side to play against. They certainly wouldn't have been our choice of opposition for such a crucial match.

Because of the one-off nature of the game, and the fact it was being played on a Friday night, the match was generating a lot of interest throughout the country. Clubs had a lot to gain by us losing, and I knew I had to do my best to stay calm in the days leading up to the match and set an example to the younger lads. This was a huge game – as big as they come – and the last thing I needed on the night before was to be targeted by match-fixers.

In an era long before the internet you didn't really hear about match-fixing. Sure, there would be the odd dodgy result, or a performance that was too bad to be true, but that's football – isn't it? To prove that someone had actually thrown a game would have been impossible. I had never heard of match-fixing from any player I had played with and I would have punched anyone's lights out if I suspected that they were willing to chuck a game. I may have been the joker, but football meant everything to me, and it would have been too much to take to work like a slave all week only for someone to affect the result.

At the same time, I wasn't naïve; I knew there were a lot of bad guys out there, and that there were certain people you didn't get on the wrong side of. I may have come from Workington, but I knew the way things worked, and that criminals would use any enterprising scheme they could dream up to make a fast buck. Gambling was one lucrative way of generating cash, and even though football betting wasn't as big a deal as it is now, it was seen as another way to extract some money from the bookies. I suppose if you are going to try to nobble the result of a game, then the best person after the referee to try to influence would be the goalkeeper. I just never thought anybody would be daft enough to try it on with me.

On the Thursday night before the Palace v Burnley game, I was sitting watching television in the house, when my telephone rang. I picked it up, and on the other end of the line was someone with a Geordie accent. 'Is that John Burridge?' he asked. 'Yes,' I said, none the wiser. 'If Crystal Palace lose tomorrow, you could be a rich man. I'm right outside your house just now. Tell me there's a chance they might lose, and in 10 minutes' time there will be £25,000 sitting on your doorstep. Come outside and pick up the parcel. It's yours.'

I really didn't know what to think. My first reaction was that it must be somebody having a joke. Maybe someone deciding to have a wind-up at my expense? After all, I'd played enough jokes on other people.

But I wasn't going to hang around to find out. I blurted out two words, the second of which was 'OFF'. I hung up the phone on him and that was the last of it. I half-expected the guy to ring back and try again, but he'd got the message.

I put it to the back of my mind and never mentioned it to anyone. To this day, I don't know if I was the only one in the team to get a call like that. Or whether people involved in other games were targeted in that way. I honestly don't know whether it was someone trying to influence the game for gambling purposes, or whether it was someone determined to make sure that Sunderland went up to the First Division. It would have been pointless for me to go running to Terry about it or going to the FA. For one, I'm no snitch. And anyway, how the hell would I have proved it anyway? It was only a voice on the other end of the phone. It didn't affect me in any way before the game; I just put it down to a crank call and went on with preparing for a massive match where I had to make sure I would be at the very top of my game.

The lads were brilliant in the hours before the game, completely focused, and on Friday, 11 May, 1979, we went out there determined not just to win the point that would deliver us into the First Division, but to beat Burnley and go up as the champions we believed we were. I had friends and family down, and Janet's mum and dad were there in an amazing crowd of 51,482. There were thousands more locked out, I don't know where they all came from. But what a noise they made inside Selhurst Park that night.

It was a horribly uncomfortable game to be part of as a goalkeeper, because we had all the possession and pressure, and I just had to stand there and keep my concentration and hope that we could break Burnley down. I was kicking every ball and I leapt for joy when we got the goal that would put one hand on the Second Division trophy with just 14 minutes to go. Vince Hilaire sent over a cross from the right, and Ian Walsh got on the end of it to head us one-up. It was party time, and Dave Swindlehurst put the icing on the cake with a second. We'd done it, we'd come from fourth to grabbing the championship in the last 14 minutes of our season.

The Palace team that night was: Burridge, Hinshelwood, Sansom, Kember, Cannon, Gilbert, Nicholas, Murphy, Swindlehurst, Walsh, Hilaire.

It was a wonderful story – young boys of 18 had helped us win the title. I'd done it with my dicky shoulder and we were going up to the First Division.

CHAPTER 11
THE PIONEER

*'My dedication far outweighed anyone else.
What is regarded as normal today, I was doing in the
late 1970s, yet I was regarded as a bit of a weirdo
at the time.'*

To prepare for life back in the top flight, it had been arranged for Palace to go to Florida for their pre-season, where they would play against North American Soccer League sides like the Tampa Bay Rowdies. Terry Venables was very friendly with Rodney Marsh, who was playing for them at the time, and that's how the game came about. American soccer was massive at that time, and superstars like Pelé, George Best and Franz Beckenbauer were playing there. I would have loved to have gone there and seen all the razzmatazz first hand, but I couldn't because I had to have my injury operated on urgently. I went to a private clinic to have my tendons fixed in my shoulder, and on the same day I checked in to go under the knife, the rest of the squad flew off to Fort Lauderdale to play Tampa Bay.

I really would love to have gone there, but I had no option – my thoughts had to fully be on next season and getting myself 100 per cent fit to be part of it. I needed a lot of recuperation and physio treatment to get myself fit, and it was a major relief when

I got the sling off after the op. I was very frightened at first that my shoulder was never going to be the same again. I'd had a few broken fingers and bust my nose more times than I cared to remember, but this was the first serious injury I had and you start to worry about the long-term effect it might have on you. But once I started swimming in the rehabilitation pool, the doubts started to ease and I had a tremendous sense of relief that I'd be able to play again. Between the end of one season and the start of another you only got six weeks off, but I was counting the days down like a kid does waiting for Santa Claus to come. I couldn't wait to get started again, and to play with this young exciting team in the First Division.

A few of the Palace players were already getting picked for England, Ireland and Wales and I was being touted for an international call-up too after the form I had shown in our promotion-winning season. Because I hadn't been playing in the First Division it had counted against me, but now that we were going up it seemed like I was going to get my chance because Ron Greenwood, the England manager at that time, had been seriously considering me and taking a close look at me. Terry was telling me: 'Budgie, you play like that again next season and I promise you you'll be getting an England spot.' It was easier said than done, of course, because Peter Shilton and Ray Clemence were dominating the No.1 jersey at the time, so the competition was fierce.

When Palace came back from Florida, one of the first things I needed to do was to see Terry Venables about my salary, because I thought I deserved a rise. I was on a two-year contract and was coming to the end of it. I'd just had one of the best seasons of my life, letting in only 24 goals in 42 league games, so I felt I was in a fairly strong bargaining position. Palace were splashing the cash on the back of their promotion

– they had bought Mick Flanagan from Charlton for
£650,000, and Gerry Francis from QPR for a million – huge
money for 1979. I was on £500 a week, and as soon as I heard
that they were on £1,000 a week and had got big signing-on
fees, I was knocking on Terry's door. I said: 'Look, Terry, I
helped win you promotion; I put up with cortisone injections
and played through the pain barrier for you. I want a £25,000
signing-on fee and a new contract and I want to be on the same
wages as them.'

I suppose I lost my temper a little bit, but while Mick and
Gerry had both played well for their respective teams, I had
played well for Palace and I thought that deserved to be
recognised. Like I said, I think the goalkeeper is the most
important position on the pitch, and that I deserved to be on a
par with the top earners. Terry was a bit taken aback, and he
pointed out to me that I still had the best part of a year left on
my contract. I wanted an extension to that deal, on better
wages, and when he knocked that back I exploded. In the heat
of the moment, I snapped at him: 'Fine, get yourself another
goalie.' I said to him that if he wanted me to play that season
and be happy, Palace should give me the money I was asking
for. Terry was always Mr Cool in those situations and, to his
credit, he said he would speak to the board and get back to me.
But when he did that, it wasn't the news I wanted to hear – he
said they had heard him out and listened to my terms, but they
couldn't do it.

It was the days before Bosman, and I knew I had to be
ruthless as I was the only one who could do something about
it. My nose was well out of joint and I told Terry I didn't want
to be at Palace, and that I wanted a move. The impasse lasted
a few days, but eventually Palace dug into their pockets thanks
to Terry's diplomacy and I got what I wanted. I got the year's

contract, I got the signing-on fee, got the salary matched to the top men. I admit I was selfish when it came to money. My philosophy was simple – if I felt I'd had a really good season then I always wanted a rise or a new contract. Basically I was adopting the 'Bosman' approach before it came in.

The rules of employment were all wrong and stacked against players in the 1970s and '80s. It was the only job in the world where you could come to the end of your contract and then your employer could keep you there and demand compensation for you. I'm glad Jean-Marc Bosman took it to the European courts and won, but back then I was doing what he later made famous, and winning. If I thought I was one of the best players at the club then I wanted to be one of the best paid – why should goalkeepers be any different? I know it sounds mercenary, and it will probably upset some fans who appreciate a bit of loyalty, but footballers have a short working life and you have to gather in as much money as you possibly can while you're playing. I felt I deserved a decent wage, given my dedication to football and my professionalism. At Palace, one night week all the lads would go out for a good drink, but not me. I'm not acting all prim and proper here and frowning at the rest of the lads' behaviour – each to their own – but I was never into that. My night was watching *Top of the Pops* and a good night's sleep. My dedication far outweighed anyone else in the team.

We started the season impressively, picking up where we had left off in the Second Division, and really underlined our potential as the new kids on the block when we faced Ipswich Town in September. They were managed by Bobby Robson, God rest his soul, and their line-up included players like Russell Osman, Terry Butcher, George Burley, Eric Gates and Paul Mariner – they were just a fantastic team. I had a good pre-season behind me, my shoulder felt strong, and I was pumped up at the thought of playing in the First Division again. I was also well pleased with my signing-on fee and contract, so I was one very happy goalie. Terry Venables had gone up even further in my estimations – here I had a great manager whom I really respected and it wasn't lost on me that he'd had to fight the board tooth and nail to get me the contract I wanted. He had taken all my cheek as well, when a lot of the time he would probably have been well within his rights to tell me to get lost. Terry Venables always went that extra yard for me.

I remember that Ipswich game for a lot of reasons. We had recently been in Bilbao to play a friendly in a tournament, in which Dynamo Moscow were also taking part. I was spellbound as I watched the Moscow goalkeeper before the game – he had been out on the field on his own to do a warm-up. This was in the days when everyone stayed in the dressing room until five to three and any warm-up was done within those four walls. I had been watching him and taking mental notes, thinking to myself: 'That's brilliant – I'm going to start doing that!' So, against Ipswich Town I came out more than half an hour before kick-off and the old groundsman at Selhurst Park was telling me: 'You can't go out now, you're not allowed on the field!'

He kept on at me, determined to clear me off the pitch, telling me: 'You're not allowed a ball.' So I said to him: 'No ball, no problem.' I had done a lot of gymnastics at school, somersaults and stretches and so on, so seeing as I couldn't have the ball I started walking on my hands across the penalty box and doing somersaults. Word had got to Terry Venables in the dressing room about what was going on, and he came out to see what the commotion was. It would be no big deal today.

Everyone is out there now doing stretches, but in 1979 there was Terry looking at me and thinking my head must have gone as he stood there watching me bouncing about doing somersaults. He was worried I'd do my back in! From then on it used to become part of my pre-match routine. I came back into the dressing room after 20 minutes, and Terry asked me if I was all right. But even then his revolutionary mind was working overtime and the more he thought about it, the more he thought it was brilliant.

In that game, I was so happy that when we went 1-0 up, I did a back somersault in my box. When we banged in a second goal I did it again. The crowd thought it was fantastic that I'd be doing somersaults every time we scored a goal, and I was kept busy entertaining them that afternoon because we were running riot. We got a third, then a fourth goal, and I thought: 'I've got to something that's going to make the fans REALLY cheer,' so I climbed up onto the crossbar and sat there – Budgie by name, Budgie by nature. I was sitting there grinning, on the corner between the bar and post, at the stanchion. I was taking the piss out of Ipswich and their striker Paul Mariner was looking at me open-mouthed, at this nutcase sitting on the crossbar. I was shouting over to the rest of the lads: 'I've got the best seat in the house – you get a cracking view from up here!' But then one of the Ipswich players tried a shot from just inside our half and I had to jump down and save it. If my manager had been Ron Saunders he would have had me strung up on that crossbar, but Terry Venables came up to me at the end of the game and said: 'That was the funniest thing I've seen in football in my life.' To this day I don't know why I did it, I just did. You would get into all sorts of problems with the FA now for unsporting conduct and all that politically correct nonsense, but I just did it to send the fans home smiling. They couldn't have been any happier to be honest – we'd just thrashed one of the best sides in the country 4-1 and Crystal Palace had gone top of the First Division for the first time in the club's history.

A few games later we were away to Manchester United at Old Trafford. You come out of the tunnel at Old Trafford in the corner at the Stretford End and everyone was looking a bit uptight as we prepared to come out on to the pitch. My way of easing the tension was to walk out of the tunnel, then across the box in front of the Stretford End, on my hands! The United fans and players were wondering what was going on, but I was only warming myself up to play a football game. It didn't do us any harm as we got a 1-1 draw.

After that, my acrobatics became the centrepiece of my regular pre-match ritual. I'd be quite happy out there on my own, and because a lot of the groundsmen wouldn't let me onto their pitch until kick-off, I'd get round that by staying off the field and doing my routine behind the goals so they couldn't stop me. After a while, Terry started to think about what I was doing and decided it would be good for the whole team to go out at 2.30 to warm up. So Crystal Palace were trailblazers by becoming the first team to come out onto the football field half an hour before a game. Our old groundsman wasn't happy with the situation – he was old school and didn't like anyone messing about with his own long-established rules. It had dawned on Terry that it made a lot of sense for players to get a feel of the ball and a feel of the pitch before kick-off. He would get the centre-forward to take shots at me, all stuff that's still done to this day. Other teams started copying us and it became the norm. It became common practice, but because I had done it first I was regarded as a bit of a freak, an extrovert, an oddball – but the truth of the matter is that I was simply thinking ahead of my time. And time has proved me right, just look at the methods used by the top clubs now.

I remember another time we played Nottingham Forest, just before Christmas 1979. Forest had won the European Cup the year before and had a very strong side. We played them at Selhurst Park and they had Peter Shilton in goal, who was the England goalkeeper at the time. Just having him in the opposite goal helped me raise my game and I played great that day. We won it 1-0 and it was another big feather in our cap. All the lads were in the mood to celebrate and headed down to the players' lounge afterwards for a couple of well-earned beers. But while they were all showered and changed and knocking back lagers in the warmth of the stadium, I was out on the pitch on my lonesome, going through my warm down and getting rid of any tension in my muscles.

Terry had seen me out on the pitch doing my stuff and then running round the track, and when I was changing in the dressing room on my own, the door opened and Terry stuck his head round. 'Budgie,' he said to me, 'I wouldn't even swap you for their keeper.' That meant everything to me, made me feel so big, so fantastic. I thought to myself, if I'm ever a manager that's the way I want to be. With just a few sincere words, he had built up my self-belief. It was just another example of Venables' man-management genius. You may think I am going overboard in my praise of the man, but I can't speak too highly about Terry Venables – he was absolutely fantastic for me. Instead of branding me a nutcase, like most people did, he used to let me get on with my eccentricities. He would accept them as long he saw that I was playing well. He accepted me for what I was. He was quite happy to go along with my revolutionary ideas.

I used to try anything that would get my mind focused on

the game. I went to what they now commonly refer to as a sports psychologist. A lot of athletes use them these days, and there is nothing unusual about using their services to get you in the zone. Clubs pay psychologists thousands now on a regular basis. But in the early 1980s they were regarded with great suspicion – they were seen as 'psychiatrists', and I think everyone thought I was a bit mental for going to see him.

As was pretty much always the case, I didn't give a toss what other people thought of my quirks, so I stuck at it. I went along to see him, told him my life story, about my upbringing, and I confided in him that I found it confusing why I could be strong in my mind one week, then a bit defeatist the next. He told me that it's all down to body rhythms – he explained it to me, broke it all down and it made perfect sense. This guy was brilliant for me. During our sessions, we decided that a course of hypnotherapy might also benefit me. He couldn't just click his fingers and put you under, it's not as simple as that; you've got to WANT to be hypnotised. I just wanted to be strong-minded every week, so I was willing to give it a go. He went ahead and hypnotised me. I had six two-hour sessions, which cost me £1,500 – and if I told anyone that at the time, they thought I was most definitely mad! The therapist would tell me a story then put me to sleep. He made me a motivational cassette as well and people used to laugh at me, because on the way to games on the team bus I'd slam it into my personal stereo and listen to the tape. I was in a trance-like state, but I could hear the boys taking the piss and calling me 'Alice in Wonderland'. But I was totally calm, and my mind was in the perfect place. Whenever I was playing – especially a big game at Anfield or Old Trafford – I wasn't nervous in the slightest, because in my thoughts I'd already been there and conquered any lingering anxiety I might have had. I was mentally ready for anything.

It became an essential part of my pre-match build-up – everything needed to be perfect in my mind when I was preparing for a game. I'd dabble in a bit of meditation too – and no matter what abuse I was getting from the lads in the background, I'd be able to shut them out of my mind and concentrate on the job in hand. What is regarded as normal today, I was doing in the late '70s and early '80s, yet I was regarded as a bit of a weirdo at the time. Having a manager like Terry helped me believe in what I was doing, because he encouraged all this. Other managers would have just dismissed me as a headcase and ordered me to stop doing it, but he recognised that there was method in my madness.

Terry kept pushing me to Ron Greenwood, saying that I deserved an England call-up, and although I didn't get any full England caps I was in the squad for select games against Holland, China and Australia.

Although I'd missed out on a trip to the United States with Palace while I was getting my shoulder sorted, I made up for it later in my career by taking Janet and the kids there for our holidays. Naturally, I couldn't switch off from football – and by watching 'soccer' in the States I drew a lot of inspiration for some of my tricks, like sitting on the crossbar. I just loved the way they presented their sports events and all the showmanship involved. It was outrageous but it put some fun into the game. I would go and see Tampa Bay Rowdies games, and I used to train with them while I was there. What the Americans were doing in the 1970s and early '80s is similar to what Sky Sports are doing now, adding a bit of glamour and razzmatazz. Football is meant to be an entertainment industry after all. Yes, first and foremost it's a professional game and you need to win, but if you can add a bit of entertainment to the mix then the paying public are getting a smile on their faces. Everyone loves a jackass. If you're the type of player that just goes out there all serious, keeps his mouth shut, and keeps himself to himself, then no one is ever going to remember you. I didn't want to be like that, I wanted to be a showman. If you're a bit of a jackass and you've got the guts to go out and do something a bit different then I would say go out and do it – stand out from the crowd. At the end of the day you have to win the game, but if you can win it with all the trimmings then it's so much sweeter. Give those fans something to remember. But the thinking towards me in the seventies was that I was an idiot – a show-off. I wasn't like that at all though, it was just charisma, and I was never big-headed, because I always knew that you were only as good as your last game.

Everything I did was dedicated to making myself a better goalkeeper and doing well for the team, but the trimmings were important to me too. I was always looking for that little something different that might make me that bit better. To give you an example – nobody ever thought about diet in those days, but I would always find out what was good for you, when was the right time to eat it, and doing my homework on sports science and nutrition. I even studied the diet of African tribesmen to try to work out the secrets of their strength and agility. Players would usually eat fish and chips or a sandwich before a game, but I thought to myself that can't be right for football. I thought there had to be something better.

I was always questioning things. I wasn't always right, but a lot of the time I was decades ahead of my time. I was the first one to be blending apples, oranges and pears and drinking it before a game – that's known as a smoothie now, but it was just dismissed as 'Budgie's strange brew' then. They used to think I was crazy, but I would actually take my blender along to the ground, go to the kitchen and make myself a cocktail packed with sugar and goodness. That would be my pre-match dinner. I'd also make sure I ate plenty of carbohydrates, including jars of baby food, which as you know are full of vitamins and iron. People used to disagree, saying: 'Don't eat potatoes, don't eat pasta,' but I'd looked into it and realised it was the best thing to give you reserves of energy. Players would be tucking into a big fat steak, but I didn't want one – it made me feel bloated, so I would do my own thing. I was regarded as a nutter for eating pasta or having a glass of water instead of a cup of tea. I didn't do it just for the sake of being different; it was all done for the sake of playing well. And while me doing somersaults might have been frowned upon, I only did it to entertain people. The fans were paying good money to be entertained, and I was only too happy to oblige them. I wouldn't have done it if we were losing right enough, because I would have looked a fool, and I always understood that the bottom line is that you have to win.

Another important thing I added to my repertoire was that I would always run to the fans at the end of a match. I especially did it away from home. Palace used to get a massive travelling support. When we used to go up north, sometimes 5,000 fans had followed us up there. I would get down on my knees in front of them and blow them kisses. Some players used to just walk off and not acknowledge the fans, but I would never have done that. I used to run from one end of the ground to the other where our fans were. The way I saw it, people had paid a lot of money to come up from London and follow us. I used to cajole all the other players to go over and do the same, and to be fair most of them did. I did this throughout my career. An extract from the *Herald* newspaper in 1992, when I played a game for Hibs at Dunfermline, nicely sums up the way I would behave:

Off-stage, the star of the afternoon was John Burridge. Hibernian's goalkeeper had nothing to do and he did it with incessant gusto. He was never still. He paced his area like a caged leopard. He did bending exercises. His tongue never stopped. He was always waving and shouting. When he ran out of other occupations, he re-dug the trench he had made at a right angle to the goal-line out to the penalty spot. It was hard to keep the eyes off Burridge.

Conspicuously, he was the only Hibernian to go and salute the travelling supporters at the end. He made so thorough a job of it that before he had completed his tour most of the fans had drifted away. Burridge was unabashed. He continued to applaud what the late Eddie Waring in a rugby commentary once called the 'empty crowd'.

There was nothing false about it; I always did it from the bottom of my heart. Mind you, if we'd just been beaten three or four-nil, I needed the hide of a rhino to go over and see the fans at the end of the game. But I was never the type to only sing when we were winning; it wasn't the result I was reacting to, it was the fact the fans had paid their money to watch their team. The fans get a raw deal in football all the time and are still taken for granted, so to go over and say thanks for their support wasn't much to ask.

When I was at Palace, football was changing rapidly and I was keen to be at the forefront of any changes. We had been over in Bilbao for a tournament and I'd seen a keeper try these new gloves. We were still mainly using our bare hands in dry weather – which may seem unthinkable now because you wouldn't see any keeper without gloves these days – but this foreign keeper was ahead of his time and had gloves that he would wear in dry weather as well as wet. After the game, I went up to the keeper and asked him all about his gloves. They had special grips and were made of latex, whereas the ones we used on a wet day were woolly. They were fantastic for catching the ball. There were still no gloves available in England like that so I got on to Terry and asked for some, badgering him to get me a batch. I was the first keeper in England to wear them on a dry day.

It quickly caught on and before long every keeper in the country was suddenly wearing gloves on a dry day. I had found out where they were made and I rang Adidas in Germany to sort out some supplies. They were £25 a pair – a lot of money for 1979 – so I asked for Terry to go the board and get them to agree to order £500-worth. At first, I was the envy of other keepers in the league – I started getting calls at my house from Peter Shilton and Pat Jennings asking me where I had got them. You'll no doubt have heard all the stories about Pat Jennings having big hands like shovels, but he actually came to my house to try them on and when he put his hands in the gloves, they were just normal size – it was all a myth. What a disappointment! Word was getting round and all the keepers were turning up at my house to get them. If I'd thought about it I could have patented them in England and made a fortune.

I remember we were playing against West Ham one day and Mervyn Day was in goal. We beat them 1-0 and Mervyn made a right howler. Straight after the game, I went up to him with a pair of gloves and said: 'Try these, son.' He thought I was being a smartarse, taking the piss out of him after his mistake, but I was only trying to do him a favour. Adidas had cottoned on, and were giving me extra pairs to pass on to other keepers because I was promoting their product. It got to the stage where I was giving the opposition keeper gloves at the end of every game. After that they started coming into the shops and were freely available to buy, but I was the first one to ring Germany and get a box sent to England. I broke the mould. It was the end of goalkeepers playing with bare hands.

CHAPTER 12
PAIN ON PLASTIC

*'Queens Park Rangers turned their pitch into an
airport runway.'*

I had a fantastic time at Crystal Palace, playing under a great
manager, but then the team started to lose a bit of its sparkle.
We had risen to the top of the First Division in the early weeks,
and we were even being tipped to make an unlikely challenge for
the title, but the big boys – Liverpool, Man United, Arsenal and
Ipswich – had the experience we lacked, and we started to get
bogged down a bit in mid-table.

The First Division was hard, and it was impossible for a team
like Palace to be winning every week. Terry was still doing some
brilliant work, but there was tension simmering at boardroom
level and it was seeping into the team's performances. We
finished the season 13th, which was a bit of a disappointment
after hitting such dizzy heights in the early months. I was
involved in another pay dispute at the start of the 1980/81
season, and morale at Palace plunged further when the club let
Kenny Sansom go to Arsenal, receiving Clive Allen and a rival
keeper, Paul Barron, in exchange – a terrible bit of business.

The man behind the unnecessary meddling was our chairman Raymond Bloye, a butcher from Croydon. The Palace fans still blame him for not realising what a good thing he had at that time and failing to invest in the club. Terry was looking for more money to allow the club to realise its true potential, and rumours and reports were flying about that he was starting to get disillusioned with the lack of encouragement he was getting at boardroom level. Everything was in place for Palace to be massive – big crowds, a team packed with brilliant young players who had won two FA Youth Cups a couple of years earlier – but it all started to turn sour. The 1980/81 season started badly and we chalked up a run of seven successive losses.

One day I picked up the newspaper and Terry had gone – he was going to take over from Tommy Docherty as the new manager of QPR in west London. You might have thought I would have seen it coming, but it was all very sudden. Sometimes that happens in football; one day a manager is there and then, without the slightest warning, you turn up at training the next day and he's gone. I was gutted to see him go.

Our coach Ernie Walley took charge of the team on a caretaker basis for a few games, and did reasonably well, but in truth he was never going to be high-profile enough to become Venables' permanent replacement. The man they eventually chose to fill Terry's shoes was a familiar face at Selhurst Park – Malcolm Allison, who'd been manager of the club between 1973 and 1976 before Terry had started his four-year reign. 'Big Mal' was a good manager, but was a bit flash for me and wasn't as dedicated as Terry. I had my own ways, and I was used to being allowed to get on with them under Terry, but Malcolm was a little bit old-fashioned and he would start to question my methods a little bit and this made me feel a little bit insecure. I became unhappy with him because I was no longer getting my own way. I played on for a month or two, then one night I got a call from a middle-man asking me: 'Would you be interested in going to QPR with Terry Venables?' The thought of working with Terry again appealed to me, and I said I would love to.

A few days later at training, Malcolm Allison called me over and said Terry had asked to see me. QPR were in the Second Division, and their goalkeeper was Chris Woods, the England under-21 international, so I wondered why they would want me. But Terry was keen on bringing me to Loftus Road, having worked with me and trusted me at Palace. Chris went off to Norwich City and I was bought as a straight replacement. I took it as quite a compliment that Terry had bought me for a second time – it showed that he valued me and had faith in me. Terry would later try to sign me when he was manager of Tottenham and I was at Southampton, but that was one deal that couldn't be finalised.

When I met Terry to thrash out the QPR deal, I quickly sorted out my salary, but I also asked for a signing-on fee, in cash, before I signed. Again, it was a case of me trying to make as much money as I could from my career – not only for me, but for Janet and the family. Terry said he had to speak to the chairman, which would be no picnic because the owner of QPR at that time was Jim Gregory, who had a reputation for being a man you didn't mess with. He reminded me a bit of the character Bob Hoskins played in *The Long Good Friday*! Terry fixed up a meeting between the three of us to sort it out, so I headed to Loftus Road to see him in his office. Gregory wasn't a very tall man, but he had this big massive swivel chair, which I think he used to make him appear physically bigger. He didn't waste any time getting down to business.

'There's your contract and there's your signing-on fee,' he said, as he laid a bag down in front of me. Inside, there were five bundles of cash. I said: 'Mr Gregory, no disrespect, but I had agreed on an amount with Terry.' 'Take it or leave it,' he said. 'Okay then, I'll leave it.'

So I got up and started to walk towards the door of his office, with my back to him, worried he was going to come flying after me and wondering already if I'd made a massive mistake for the sake of a few readies. It was all about saving face, though. I couldn't turn round, I would have looked pathetic. As soon as I put my hand on the door handle, he said: 'John, come back.' He opened the drawer and chucked another bundle of cash on the table. He had been testing me, and although my heart was pounding it had been worth digging my heels in. I signed the contract there and then in his office, took my money and off I went – with my nerves shot to pieces.

I had arrived halfway through the season and QPR were near the bottom of the Second Division. Terry had quickly worked his magic the moment he was in the door, winning his first three games and guiding QPR up to eighth by the end of the 1980/81 season – nothing short of remarkable given the dire position they had been in before he was appointed. He already had guys like Glenn Roeder and Simon Stainrod in place, but soon he bought players of the calibre of Terry Fenwick and Gerry Francis and started to put a very useful side together.

But for some unknown reason that summer QPR decided to rip up their turf and put a plastic pitch down in its place. I couldn't understand it. They grabbed all the headlines for being innovative and at the cutting edge of technology, but it didn't make any sense to me. I was preparing for an exciting new season and hopefully a promotion push, and we were getting some really good players through the doors for the season ahead – including John Gregory from Brighton, Clive Allen and Mike Flanagan from Palace.

Terry had proved he could build a good team and get them playing well so everything looked set up for us to have a brilliant season. But then they put down that synthetic surface – becoming the first club in England to put down an artificial pitch. I wasn't keen on the idea, but I tried to keep an open mind. It wasn't long before my mind was made up 100 per cent though, because the first time I went out onto the pitch I found it was like concrete. I was thinking to myself: 'They've turned the pitch into an airport runway and they expect us to play on that?'

The rumour was that the board were also planning to put a roof over the pitch. Loftus Road was a beautiful stadium. It wasn't the biggest, but it was a nice compact ground. Jim Gregory was a businessman and had the idea of creating an arena that could host big concerts featuring all the big acts at that time – Tina Turner, the Rolling Stones or big boxing bouts. Instead of the stadium being used just once a fortnight to host QPR games, they were talking about the ground being in continuous use, with amateur players renting it for five-a-sides. But they didn't get planning permission to go the whole hog.

There was a whole lot of talk about how good the artificial pitch was, but for me it just seemed like propaganda. All the big plans being spouted for Loftus Road were turning the club into a bit of a circus and for a while it felt like football was playing second fiddle. Jim Gregory may have been a brilliant businessman, and he had many grand plans, but I didn't like that side of it whatsoever. I just wanted to concentrate on the football club, get them into the First Division, and kick on from there.

PAIN ON PLASTIC

I gave it a go on the artificial pitch for about six months, but it was hellish. We'd be playing one week on the plastic pitch and then the next away from home on grass, and it was becoming difficult to adjust from one week to the next. It got to the stage where I used to hate playing at home. Football is meant to be played on grass. The plastic pitch of 1981 was light years away from the artificial surfaces we have today. Those types of pitches have now come on in leaps and bounds, and a lot of them now are almost as good as grass. But in 1981 it was an altogether different story – a plastic pitch was just a thin carpet plonked down on concrete.

The ball used to bounce ridiculously high. When you dived on it your body used to ache. I would be scarred and gashed to pieces. I had carpet burns all over the place from the synthetic surface and it would take me days at a time to recover fully. It wasn't much fun for outfield players, but for goalkeepers it was brutal. Your elbows had to be padded, your thighs had to be padded; you ran out looking like Robocop because you had so much protective gear stuffed under your shirt and tracksuit bottoms. When you got knocked over, you came down hard. Because it was the 1980s, and there seemed to be a new invention every week, I think a lot of fans embraced it at first. But after they had watched a few matches and seen the ball bouncing all over the place, with the players running about in trainers and struggling to control the ball, they started to have some reservations. I think it was mainly brought in as a way of copying the Americans. But in the US Soccer League, they would be playing in enclosed arenas in the Florida heat. A wet and windy day in west London wasn't quite the same. It was so dangerous to play on, and I wasn't happy on it at all. A lot of the lads suffered in silence, but keeping my mouth shut was never my style and I started to voice my concerns to Terry. I told him that a pitch like that would take years of the life expectancy of a player, and especially a keeper. I reckoned if you played on that week-in week-out it would take five or six years off your career. You had players complaining of bad backs, bad knees and bad ankles because of the pounding their bodies took on it – and I can't remember a single voice speaking up in support of it. It got to the stage where I'd had enough, and I told Terry I couldn't keep playing on it. I launched into a tirade against plastic pitches. Terry told me: 'Budgie, I hear what you are saying, but you can't go saying that in the papers.' But I had the bit between the teeth and I said: 'I can and I will.' And I did.

I started being heavily critical publically, airing my views in no uncertain terms to the press whenever the opportunity presented itself. I made the point that in every training session a keeper would be coming down a thousand times on it. My body was taking a battering, but the board were happy enough to keep the dreaded plastic because other teams hated it too and we rarely lost at home. After I'd had my say in the papers, I then asked to be put on the transfer list. It was tough in a football sense to walk away from a club managed by Terry Venables, but I knew I was fighting a losing battle. I could slate the surface as much as I liked to the press, it wasn't going to be enough to persuade the Queens Park Rangers board to change their minds and go back to a grass pitch. The directors saw me as a troublemaker and the atmosphere towards me was frosty. They thought that because they paid my wages I should shut up and get on with it. They clearly didn't know me very well.

I needed to get away from the artificial turf as quick as I possibly could, so I could enjoy my football again, and so to bring matters to a head I refused to play on it any more. My

WORKINGTON TOWN FOOTBALL CLUB 1970

LEFT TO RIGHT :- J.LATTIMER (Trainer), R.WOOD, I.MASSIE, J.BURRIDGE, T.GERMINTIS, M.HOGAN, J.OGILVIE, T.SPENCER, B.DOYLE (Manager),
MIDDLE ROW :- J.MARTIN, D.HELLIWELL, J.WILSON, D.BUTLER, J.GOODFELLOW, T.SPRATT, A.TYRER,
FRONT ROW :- D.IRVING, D.SHIELDS, K.WOOKEY.

Above: A baby-faced Budgie with Workington Reds in 1967/68. I must have been one of the smallest in the team at that stage!

Below: By 1970, I had broken into the first team, and was mixing it with some hard cases in the old Fourth Division.

Above left: My unique training regime started to take shape at Blackpool.

© *Blackpool Gazette*

Above right: The pressure was always on with ambitious Aston Villa. © *Getty Images*

Below: With the rest of the Villa lads and the League Cup in 1977. © *Getty Images*

Above: Another sunny day in south London – in goal for Crystal Palace in 1979, where I played under my favourite manager and mentor, Terry Venables. © *Getty Images*

Left: The 1978/79 Second Division Championship was a thriller, but we got our hands on the trophy.

Above: I would take on and beat all-comers when it came to hard training.

Below left: An acrobatic save from my QPR days in 1981 – but I hated their plastic pitch.

Below right: I was happy to be fed to the Wolves in 1982. Here I am posing with Kenny Hibbitt.

© Getty Image.

bove: Shouting instructions to my defenders (as usual!) in goal for Wolves in 1983.

elow: 1985 saw a move to Southampton (below left) and then it was on to
ɪeffield United (below right) – but only after a bizarre escape through Arthur
ɔx's window!

Above left: At Newcastle in 1990. I loved the club, but Ossie Ardiles kicked me ou

Above right and below: Playing for Hibernian at the age of 40 was one of the best periods of my career, and I helped deliver the Skol League Cup to Easter Road in 1991.

never missed a chance to say thank you to the supporters. Here I am saluting the Aberdeen fans in 1995.

My new life in the Middle East. Having a laugh with my protégé Ali Al-Habsi in Oman and, dressed as sharp as ever, here I am in the TV studio alongside Joe Morrison on Ten Sports.

©VK Shafeer and Ten Spor

relationship with Terry suffered over that, because I had gone against his wishes and voiced my opinion to the press after he had advised me it wouldn't be a good idea. But for me I was only telling the truth and trying to stand up for the players. What I said was what every other player was thinking.

I eventually got my wish; I got a move away from QPR but on loan first of all, to Wolves. Ironically, in my absence, QPR would go all the way to the FA Cup final that year, meeting and beating my former club Crystal Palace on the way, with my replacement Peter Hucker doing a good job in goal.

CHAPTER 13

IS IT A BUDGIE?
IS IT A PLANE...?

'I told the manager I was going to play in a
Superman costume.'

When I started making noises that I wanted out of QPR and away from their horrendous plastic pitch, it wasn't just Wolves who wanted to sign me. I had a couple of options. Gerry Francis had just left the club to go to Coventry City in the First Division, and he kept ringing me, telling me to come and join him. But the agreement to go on loan to Wolves was already in place, and it turned out to be a brilliant move for me.

I had a fantastic start at Molineux and we never lost a game during my first month there. I settled in really well and while I was keen to secure a permanent move away from QPR, Coventry were still sniffing about and waving the carrot of First Division football under my nose. I needed to get my future sorted fast, so I spoke to Jim Gregory and he agreed to sell me. He quickly agreed a deal with Wolves, who were willing to pay £225,000 for me – £75,000 more than Coventry's highest offer. I was dithering about Wolves, waiting to see what sort of offer Coventry would come back with, but Gregory made my mind up for me. I wasn't going to be allowed to just slip away from Loftus Road without a parting shot from the chairman, who I had really rattled with my criticism of his artificial pitch.

I was on the phone talking over my move with Terry, who was in his office at the ground, when Jim Gregory's voice burst onto the line. 'You fucking mongrel!' he snapped. 'You took that signing-on cash from me then you've got the nerve to complain about the pitch! If you don't go to Wolves like I tell you, I will make an example of you. I'll have you here for years playing for the reserves on the plastic every week!'

He slammed the phone down on me. I talked it over with Terry again. I was panicking; I was out my depth dealing with someone like Gregory. They made me suffer for two days before Terry got back to me and said he'd calmed Gregory down. 'But Budgie,' Terry added, 'I think you'd better go to Wolves like he says.'

So I signed for Wolves and although my salary came down a bit, I wasn't bothered because I was just there to play football, and to play it on grass like it should be played! I had to start looking for a house in Wolverhampton so Janet went house-hunting and found us a lovely Georgian mansion. I also found that, all of a sudden, I had a lot of free time on my hands. When I was in London it would take me ages just to drive to training in the traffic. In Wolverhampton, I could drive to the ground in five minutes. It took a bit of adjusting from the hustle-bustle and banter of London to the peace and quiet of my new home city. Wolverhampton isn't exactly a backwater, and its football team is one of the biggest clubs in the Midlands, but after London it was still very different.

The football was going very well and we had a fantastic team at Wolves – in front of me in defence were Geoff Palmer, John Pender, Alan Dodd and John Humphrey. In midfield we had guys like Kenny Hibbitt, Peter Daniel and Micky Matthews, while my long-time pal from Villa Andy Gray, Wayne Clarke and Mel Eves were up front scoring goals for fun. Wolves had just come down from the First Division and I had been bought to help get them back up there. I already had something of a reputation for helping teams win promotion, so I fitted the bill.

For Wolves, it was seen – rather naïvely as it turned out – as the dawning of a new era, because not only had they been relegated the season before, but they had been in receivership and three minutes from going out of business before the Bhatti brothers stepped in to save them. Football fans need hope to keep them going and people were full of optimism that the nightmare was behind them and that it would be a turning point. It would have been tragic if a club like Wolves went to the wall, and fans still talk about how close it came to happening. It wasn't long before the doom and gloom that had carried over from relegation and the brush with extinction lifted, and we soon had a great atmosphere in the club, with big crowds coming to Molineux in the firm belief that we would quickly get back to the First Division. We were able to fuel their optimism as we made a solid start to the 1982/83 season.

The lads at Wolves loved my dressing room antics and, looking back, I did some of the craziest things of my life at that club. They had a big old-fashioned dressing room with a rail running round it about 6ft from ground level. Above the rail, there was a spaghetti-like cluster of wires leading up to the strip lights. We had no gym at the ground, which bugged me a bit because I was really into my weights at the time. I was forced to improvise to stay in shape, so I stuck an iron bar across the rail, over the angle at the corner, so I could do my chin-ups. I got into a routine where I would do my press-ups on the floor, then my chin-ups on the bar before I went to training. I was always working on my body to keep it strong. Even before games, I would jump up on that bar and do my chins to get warmed up for the match before we went out.

One week, we were playing Oldham, and as usual I jumped up onto my bar. But after me doing hundreds of chins day after day the bar had completely worn down the wire above it and all of a sudden a shitload of volts came surging through it. I felt it zap through my body, electrifying me as I was swinging there, and I couldn't let go. I was hanging there like a crazed monkey, screaming at the top of my voice. All the lads were in fits of laughter, thinking I was having a funny turn, but the truth was I was actually frying before their eyes! I eventually managed to loosen my grip and slumped down to the ground, and when I looked at my hands they had turned blue. But there was no question of me missing the game, we didn't have anyone else, so I went out and played, probably still packed full of enough electricity to light up the city, and managed to keep a clean sheet in a 0-0 draw.

We were especially strong in defence, and looked promotion material from the word go. We were top of the league most of the season, but we had far too many draws, and my old team QPR knocked us off top spot. It would have been nice to have won the championship again, having already done it with Palace, but QPR – helped by their plastic pitch home advantage – were not for catching, and we had to settle for second spot.

We clinched promotion with two games to spare after a hell of a game against Charlton, which finished 3-3 after us being 3-0 up at half-time. We could afford to go out and enjoy our last game of the season, a home encounter against Newcastle United. I had been voted the player of the year and was due to get my award before the game, so I thought I would collect it in style. On the way to Molineux, I stopped at a fancy dress shop and I hired a Superman outfit.

Before the game, I was mucking around in the dressing room with my Superman uniform – prancing about in my blue tights and red pants. I decided to up the ante, and told the lads I was going to go out and do the warm-up with the costume on, so I out I went with the cape and mask, emerging from the tunnel with my fist out, Superman-style. It was a full house of 22,500 and the crowd were pissing themselves laughing. We took a break from the warm-up to gather in the centre circle and I was presented with my player of the year award with my fancy dress suit on.

As I warmed up, all the Newcastle players were nudging each other and pointing at me. Chris Waddle and Kevin Keegan came down towards the Wolves end, laughing and calling me an idiot. Kevin shouted over: 'It looks great, Budgie – shame you can't play in it!' That was all the encouragement I needed, and I shouted back: 'Just watch me. I bet you a hundred quid that I AM going to play in it!'

When we got into the dressing room I told the manager, Graham Hawkins, that I was going to play in it and he got a bit upset about it. The linesman would always come in about 2.45 to check the studs. There was no sponsorship in those days, so I didn't have any logo I had to display and I wasn't breaking any rules. So I asked the linesman, and he said he had no objections as long as I didn't clash with the other team. So I took off the cape, kept the tights and the blue top and taped a number one onto my back. I put a pair of proper shorts on top of my blue tights and I ran out, half-Superman, half-Wolverhampton Wanderers goalie. After the game, a 2-2 draw, Keegan was true to his word and he gave me £100 for the bet and told me that was the best entertainment he had ever seen on a football pitch.

Another costume prank I played at Wolves was at the players' Christmas party. Before the night out, there was a lot of squabbling, with the dressing room split on what we should wear – half of them wanted dicky bows and dinner suits, while the rest of them wanted to go smart, but casual. The smart but casual camp won, so I turned up in a dinner suit cut in half and sewn onto a tramp's outfit!

The Wolves supporters had been brilliant and I almost had a tear in my eye as I applauded them at the end of what had been a great season. I got on really well with the local journalist Dave Harrison and his match report afterwards in the *Wolverhampton Express and Star* quoted me as saying: 'It was a very emotional moment for me. The fans have been a 13th man for us this season and I would have liked to have gone and shaken every one of them by the hand.'

That was true – the Wolves fans were amazing. Their passion stood them in good stead, because even though they'd just bounced back to the First Division there were some incredibly dark days ahead as the Bhatti brothers turned out to be Wolves in sheep's clothing.

We went away to Majorca for an end-of-season trip to celebrate our promotion. I was not a drinker but that didn't mean I couldn't still enjoy myself on these trips. The rest of the lads had worked their arses off during the season and were entitled to get a few lagers down their necks and enjoy the sun, sea and sand, but I remained dedicated to my fitness regime – and I think that drove a few of them barmy. They would be lying on the beach chilling out, and I'd be fidgeting about, trying to get one of them to come for a run with me or do some sit-ups. I had very high fitness levels, and it didn't matter where we were, I wanted to maintain them. I wasn't the type of footballer who decided to spend the summer drinking and relaxing then turn up for pre-season ready to sweat it all off. But we had great team spirit at Wolves and it was a brilliant trip. I may not have been joining in the big rounds of drinks but I could still have some fun, and I brought the house down when all the lads were standing at the bar in a club and I walked past them on my hands in just my underpants.

Because it had been such a fantastic season and because I had played so well myself, it was time to be 'John Burridge The Greedy' again when we came back for the new season in the First Division. I felt that Wolves were going to make an awful lot of money by going up to the top flight again, so I wanted a piece of the action.

I went to see Graham Hawkins and explained to him that I had taken a serious drop in wages to come to the club in the first place, which was okay for the Second Division, but not now we'd gone up. I told him that for First Division football I wanted First Division wages. But he said there was nothing he could do – I had signed a contract and I would be expected to honour it.

The new season started, but because I hadn't been given what I wanted, I don't think my heart was really in it. My mind wasn't as focused as it should have been. Yes, I had a beautiful house and the kids were happy, but that made no difference to me, I wanted First Division wages and I became disillusioned. We were struggling in the league, too, and matters got worse in November 1983 when the club transferred my closest friend, Andy Gray, to Everton for a ridiculously cheap £250,000. Hawkins was struggling to get results and was trying anything to stop the rot, including dropping me for a while for Paul Bradshaw. I wasn't having that, and got the newspaper round to my house where I got my photo taken with all my player of the year trophies from the year before, to show who should be the Wolves No.1. I wasn't out of the team for long after that stunt. Graham Hawkins didn't last the season though – they sacked him in April, with Wolves bottom of the league and heading back to the Second Division – and called for 'The Doc', Tommy Docherty.

The salary dispute was still bugging me and after my second year at Wolves I told them I didn't want to play for them anymore. I had come to the end of my contract and it was time to move on. I had been fantastic in my first full season at Wolves, but if I'm being honest, I was no better than mediocre in my second season.

When we started pre-season training I went in to see Tommy to thrash out my future. Tommy acknowledged that I'd been good for the club and asked me to write down how much I wanted on a bit of paper. The next day I scribbled a figure down on a bit of paper, stuck it in an envelope and left it on his desk. When he saw me later that day, Tommy said: 'Fuckin' hell, who do you think you are – Gordon Banks?' It wasn't really Tommy's call on the wages though – the owners of Wolves were more intent on making cutbacks than forking money out to keep me happy.

When the season started they brought a young kid through the ranks – a guy I have always thought the world of – Tim Flowers. I had taken him under my wing and worked with him since he was 16. He used to travel from Coventry every day and I would give him lifts to and from reserve games, let him have a quick nap at our house before he played, give him some egg and toast and a cup of tea, and then go down to the ground to watch him play. When I told Tommy I wasn't going to play for the wages I was on, he was sympathetic enough. He agreed I deserved to get what I wanted, but his hands were tied, so they started young Timmy in my place, which wasn't right because he was only 17 years old.

Wolves under the Bhatti brothers were in freefall. They had put a club legend, Derek Dougan, in charge as chief executive, but that didn't mask their shortcomings. They took all the assets out of the club. There were big demonstrations at the way things were going. The fans were upset at Andy being sold, that I wouldn't play and that Wayne Clarke was going to be sold. It was clear that there was no investment; they were just stripping the club bare. Wolverhampton's ground was in the town centre, and the word on the street was that they wanted to sell the stadium and make a killing. It became pretty obvious why I couldn't get a pay rise, and I thought I was better off out of it. They were only too happy to sell me – money for me in their coffers and another senior player off the wage bill. When I wasn't playing, and they were struggling down the bottom of the league I felt sorry for them. But I had to stand my ground. I had nothing against the team though and I really loved the fans. I would pay my way into the game and go and watch it with the crowd. But attendances had dropped. It was sad, because Wolverhampton Wanderers tumbled from the First Division to the Fourth Division in successive years. It's great to see them doing well now, back in the Premier League where they belong, and with a lovely stadium, because they are a fantastic club. Jack Hayward turned them round in the 1990s and made them the proud club they are today, but the previous owners very nearly put them out of business.

CHAPTER 14

FOXY COXY

'Arthur Cox was in the central reservation, hopping mad and with a teapot in his hand, about to launch it at my car.'

For the first few weeks of the 1984/85 season I became more used to watching games than playing, but then I finally got a chance to escape from my financial stalemate at Wolves. Tommy Docherty was good friends with Arthur Cox at Derby County, and I got a call from Tommy saying Arthur was interested in taking me there on a loan deal. I agreed and thought it would be a good move to make, just to get playing again and put myself in the shop window.

Derby County were another club that had been in serious financial trouble, and they had been relegated to the Third Division in what was their centenary year. But Robert Maxwell had invested in them, and his son Ian was put in charge as chairman. I went over to see Arthur and he gave me the warmest of welcomes. He was an old-fashioned football man, and I loved his dedication. He showed me round the training ground – the Ram Arena – which was probably the best training ground I ever played on. Arthur was very clear in his vision for the club and was confident Derby County were going places. He explained to me that I was being brought in to help them with their promotion push. We started off the season very well. Derby still had some big players like Kenny Burns and John Robertson – veterans of Nottingham Forest's championship and European Cup-winning team – and Arthur had brought in a lot of new faces he was going to mould into an exciting side. I played six games for them, most of which we won, but while I was there I got a call from Ian Porterfield, the manager of Sheffield United. I was about to have my head turned.

Sheffield United were potentially a massive club, and were going well under Ian in the Second Division, and the idea of moving to a big city club really appealed to me. So, after I had played the last game of my loan deal for Derby County against Hull City, I went in to see Arthur. He had been over the moon with how I'd done and I was the blue-eyed boy because we'd kept winning during my spell on loan. He recognised that I was controlling the defence and liked my input. But when I went in to see him and told him: 'Arthur, Sheffield United want to see me on Monday,' he replied 'Don't be silly son, you're signing for us.'

It was a Saturday night when I spoke to Arthur, and I told him that I had arranged to meet Porterfield and the Sheffield United chairman Reg Brealey, who was pumping a lot of money into the club, in Nottingham on the Monday at two o'clock. 'No, you can't,' Arthur told me, as if that was the end of the matter.

We agreed to disagree, but Arthur rang me at home on the Sunday and said: 'Son, you're not going to Nottingham tomorrow, are you? I'll see you at training, eh?' I said: 'Boss, I won't be at training tomorrow. I'm going to Nottingham to

speak to Sheffield United.' He knew I had to pass Derby to get
to Nottingham from Wolverhampton, so he said 'Okay, but
pop in on the way to have a cup of tea with me.'

He phoned me again at home at 9am on the Monday to
check I was coming, so I promised him I would be there, but
again I told him I was still going to meet Porterfield and
Brealey. Arthur Cox was plain football crazy. When he wanted
a player, he wanted him bad. He was so dedicated. He will die
on a football field, and will be quite happy to go that way –
he's just like me that respect.

When I got to the Ram Arena, Arthur was waiting for me
and he beckoned me into his office. But as soon as we were
inside, he walked back over to the door, took a big bunch of
keys out of his pocket and locked the bloody door. He said:
'You're not getting out of here, you bugger, until you have
signed for Derby County.' I started laughing, thinking it was a
joke. 'But I've got to see Sheffield at two o'clock,' I protested.
'You're not going, son. I'm signing you.' He started to give me
the hard sell. 'You like me, son, don't you?' Yes. 'You like this
football club?' Yes. 'You like the supporters?' Yes.

We kept talking for about an hour and he was throwing
everything at me, urging me to sign. I was trying to reason
with him, saying I'd think about it, but I still wanted to meet
Sheffield United and hear what they had to say. But there was
no getting through to Arthur – he was miles away, his eyes
looked like they were on fire, he was so intense about it.

He started to make me an offer he thought I couldn't
possibly refuse. He wrote a figure down on a bit of paper,
offering great wages, an unbelievable package – £2,000 a week
and a signing-on fee. It was a hell of a salary, I admitted. But I
was getting twitchy and looking at the clock, which was
creeping towards one o'clock. The players were already at the

Ram Arena for training, and as they went past the window they were all giving me a wave.

In desperation, I tried to reason with him, saying that I would meet Sheffield United and then get back to him. But he wasn't listening. 'I know what you want, son, you want a car don't you?' he said. 'You can have mine!'

For a second I was tempted to take his car. He had a beautiful new Ford Granada, and told me: 'Take my car son, take it now. I can get another one from Mr Maxwell.' He phoned him while I was there sitting in the office, and told me Maxwell would give me whatever I was looking for. It was now after 1pm, and I had less than an hour to get out of there and see Ian Porterfield. Arthur hadn't taken his eyes off me, but thinking he was winning me round he dropped his guard and eventually asked 'Would you like a cup of tea and a sandwich, son?'

I said I'd love one, so off he went to the door, unlocked it and shouted up the corridor to the tea lady. But we'd been in there for so long, she'd knocked off for the day and was nowhere to be seen – so Arthur had to desert his sentry post and go off to get the tea himself, taking care to lock the door behind him.

He hadn't covered all the bases though. While he was away busy making us a cuppa, I wriggled out of his office window, ran across the car park and jumped in my car. As I pulled off, I saw his door fly open and Arthur came running towards the motor with a teapot in his hand. When you came out of the Ram Arena there was a one-way system, so you had to turn left, go along the dual carriageway then turn round and come back again. But as I drove back, there was Arthur standing in the central reservation with the teapot still in his hand. He could see I wasn't for stopping and I had to swerve to avoid knocking him down. When I looked in my mirror I could see him hopping mad, and then he let fly with the teapot, hurling it towards my car. He was raging.

When I got to the hotel in Nottingham, it had gone two. Another 20 minutes passed and there was still no sign of Ian Porterfield or anyone from Sheffield United. I was thinking to myself 'bloody typical' after what I'd gone through to get there, but then I heard a call: 'Mr Burridge to reception please.' I thought it must be Sheffield United saying they were going to be late, but it was Arthur begging me not to sign for them. I couldn't get into another conversation with him, but I was saved from more earache when Ian and Reg arrived.

I liked what Ian had to say, so we shook on it and agreed that I would go to Bramall Lane the next day to complete all the formalities for a permanent move away from Wolves.

When I got back to Wolverhampton, Janet told me Arthur had been ringing the house all day, pestering her to make sure I rang him the moment I got in. Much as I admired Derby and believed in Arthur, Sheffield United were a much bigger club with a greater history, and my mind was made up. Out of courtesy, I phoned Arthur back and he answered before it had even rung once. He was ranting on again – telling me Porterfield was doolally, that their stadium was rubbish, that kind of thing. He was doing everything he could to put down Sheffield United and make out that Derby County were the best thing since sliced bread. Eventually, he cut to the chase and said: 'So, are you signing for us then Budgie?' When I told him: 'Sorry Arthur, I've agreed to sign for Sheffield United,' there was a moment's silence, then the phone went dead. He'd hung up on me.

I had to go to Derby to fetch some of my stuff, and because they had a game on the Tuesday I thought I'd go along and watch. I spoke to John Robertson, and he arranged to leave a ticket for me. When I got into the Baseball Ground I walked down the steps to the front and shouted over to Robbo to thank him for the ticket, but just at that moment Arthur walked out from the tunnel and spotted me. It was half an hour before kick-off and there were about 10,000 people inside, but that didn't stop him walking round the track and letting rip. 'There he is, the traitor!' He'd gone crackers. He turned to the crowd and shouted: 'What do you think of the traitor? One minute he's doing somersaults for you, the next he's sticking two fingers up at you! Stewards, get him out of here!' So two stewards came along and took me out of the ground.

As it turned out, that season Sheffield United didn't win promotion. With the benefit of hindsight, I had made a bad decision. Instead of signing me, Derby County got a lad from Leicester City called Mark Wallington, who did very well. Arthur Cox's team went from strength to strength and there was a lot of ill feeling between Derby County and me. Robert Maxwell went out and spent fortunes on good players and they gained promotion after promotion. It was a terrible decision to turn someone like Arthur Cox down, who was football crazy. Not going to Derby with Arthur was probably one of the biggest mistakes I made in football because the man was an absolute winner.

About two months later, Derby were playing Doncaster Rovers away. It wasn't far away from my new home in Sheffield, so I thought I would pop down to see the game. Derby won quite easily and I thought Arthur would be quite happy. I was standing in the tunnel when the Derby lads came out and I cheerily said: 'Hello Arthur.' But instead of saying hello back, he just growled at me: 'Don't you come near me. You're cancer, I might catch it.' He then backed himself slowly along the wall, as if I was contagious. I could see in his eyes that at that moment, he actually hated me. I had crossed him, and he wasn't going to forgive me. Terry Venables was technically the best coach I ever worked for, but Arthur Cox and Kevin Keegan were by far the most enthusiastic – I used to call him Mr Football, and coming from me, that's some title!

Janet and I sold our house in Wolverhampton and moved across to Sheffield, where we moved into an even bigger property. Sheffield's famous for its steel, and the house had belonged to a tycoon who had made his fortune selling knives and forks to just about every house, hotel and restaurant in England. He had been a multi-millionaire, but had gone bankrupt and we got a tip-off from one of the Sheffield United directors that his house was being auctioned off. You had to make your offers in a sealed envelope and the next day we found out we had won – we got it for £115,000. It was an absolute mansion with big gates and it came with a snooker room, a swimming pool, a tennis court and nine bedrooms. It was like a dream come true – it was the best house I owned in my career. It was an old house and just for good measure it was meant to have a ghost. You could apparently hear noises coming from where the servants' quarters used to be. The story went that one of the servants had been thrown down the stairs by the owner a hundred years ago, and although I never heard anything myself, Janet swears she did, and sometimes heard noises coming from the stairs. All the players would come over and bring their families round on a Sunday for a bit of swimming and snooker. My house became the Sheffield United social club.

I had some good times at Sheffield United, and I used to drive my room-mate on away trips – Mel Eves – mad with my eccentric ways. He'd come up to the room on the Friday night before the game, just wanting to watch a bit of telly, and I'd be there waiting for him in my green goalkeeper's jersey, lying on my bed wanting him to throw rolled-up socks or fruit at me, using the headboard as a makeshift goal. He was just wanting to get his head down for the night and get some sleep, but I'd be screaming at him: 'Test me, Evesey!' I'd be leaping around the bed, tipping socks over the headboard, and telling him: 'Peter Shilton stopped me getting 100 caps for England!'

Evesy stayed in the same street as me in Sheffield – Riverdale Road – so I'd be driving him mad most afternoons because he was just a phone call away. When I got back from training I'd be bored and restless, so I'd call him up and drag him out to the gym I used. It was full of Hells Angels and serious bodybuilders, but they were good guys and just as dedicated as me to their fitness. I think Mel thought I was leading him to a mugging, but he got into the spirit of it!

We had a good bunch of lads at Sheffield United and the banter was good. I used to get slaughtered for the 'lucky shirt' that I wore. We weren't the type of club to wear tracksuits to away games, so we always travelled in club blazer, flannels, shirt and tie. I had a white shirt that I swear brought me luck, and I would insist on wearing it. But it was ancient and had a dirty big hole ripped right down the side, so all that was really left was the collar and the front part – like a bib! One day it was so hot on the bus, I took my jacket off and there was absolute uproar. The lads were falling about, so I started parading around and doing a few poses for them and playing to the crowd. Still kept wearing the shirt long after that though!

Another trip that raised a few laughs was when we were coming back from a challenge game in Holland. As we were walking through the airport, I noticed a couple of empty seats behind a check-in desk and jumped into one. There was a bunch of holidaymakers shuffling along behind us, so when they approached I shouted in my best official-sounding voice: 'PASSPORTS please!' They fell for it hook, line and sinker – they formed a queue and started handing their passports over to me to be checked. I was just smiling away, making polite small talk and waving them on, until I noticed one of the Sheffield United directors had joined the back of the queue. I got myself out of there pronto.

Throughout my time at Sheffield United I was playing well enough, and was an ever-present for the 1985/86 season, but as a team we weren't firing on all cylinders. I wasn't having the impact on the team I had done at Crystal Palace and QPR, and although we briefly got into the promotion spots in the first part of the season, we couldn't push on and finished seventh. It cost Ian Porterfield his job and after he was sacked they brought in another Scot, Billy McEwan.

I was still enjoying the football, training and the city of Sheffield, but I felt uneasy when I saw what was happening at Derby – the games they were winning and the players they were buying with Maxwell's millions. I could feel it gnawing away at my stomach that I'd made a mistake.

Derby were alongside us in the Second Division for 1986/87, having eased up from the Third under Arthur, and much to his satisfaction they beat us home and away on their way to winning the championship, while we limped in to a distant ninth. We had a real problem scoring goals that year. Keith Edwards had scored more than 20 the season before, but he'd been sold to Leeds and the void wasn't filled. We just never quite had the players we needed to win promotion. I tried my best for them and actually kept quite a few clean sheets, but collectively it didn't happen.

When I came to the end of my contract, for once I wasn't in

a position to ask for any more money, because we hadn't gone up – we'd failed and I'd failed, which was sad because it was the type of club with the sort of fans that deserved to be in the top league. They wanted rid of me because my wages were too high, and my old centre-half Chris Nicholl had taken over at Southampton, and when he got in touch with me it looked like Budgie was about to fly south.

CHAPTER 15
DELL BOY

*'Alan Shearer would have chased paper on a
windy day, he was so keen.'*

After Sheffield United, I had a straight choice between
moving to the south coast of England or the north-east of
Scotland because Ian Porterfield – who had taken me to Bramall
Lane in the first place – was now in charge of Aberdeen. They
had won the European Cup-Winners' Cup only four years earlier
and were still a massive club after Sir Alex Ferguson's work at
Pittodrie, so it was a tempting proposition to give Scotland a try.
The south coast option was Southampton, and I took it,
although looking at my decision from a purely financial rather
than a footballing perspective, it was one of the biggest mistakes
of my life. The North Sea oil industry was enjoying a massive
upturn and was about to send house prices in Aberdeen into
orbit. When the deal had been on the table I could have had a
castle with its own grounds and fishing rights for £200,000, and
within a couple of years it was worth nearer five million. In those
days, footballers who used their heads and wanted to make a
good living from the game would move where the house prices

were about to go up. I would have got rich quick, but I just didn't see it coming, and instead we downsized from the mansion we'd had in Sheffield and headed to Southampton.

Financially, it was a stupid mistake to go there, but the football was a big plus. I had gone from the Second Division to the First Division and it was a good opportunity for me. Chris Nicholl, my old centre-half at Aston Villa, was the manager at The Dell and he helped me get settled quickly. I had a lot to live up to though. This was one of the biggest challenges I had to face in football, because the man I was replacing was a certain Peter Shilton, who had left to join Derby County for £1 million – another big signing made with Maxwell's seemingly never-ending supply of money. Shilts had the reputation of being the best keeper in the world at that time and I arrived on the doorstep with the task of trying to assume his mantle. I knew it was a hell of a feat to take over from Peter Shilton, but Chris was a good motivator, and he took me aside and told me: 'If anyone can do it, it's you. I know your capabilities.'

Compared to some other clubs, Southampton were quite small. The fans were passionate enough, but in a coastal city like Southampton, football doesn't really take first priority. The number one interests down there were yachting and sailing, closely followed by horseriding and the country life. It was all a bit alien to a lad who had been brought up in a coal-mining village. The outlook among the fans in Southampton seemed to be that as long as the team stayed in the First Division everyone was happy. Around the same time I was arriving they brought in another young goalkeeper – the lad I had taken under my wing at Wolverhampton, Tim Flowers. They essentially bought him as one for the future, and to replace me in time. But although I was the top dog on paper, and Tim had been signed as a future prospect, I felt that my first-team place was never too secure because Tim had really matured at Wolves and was an excellent up-and-coming goalkeeper, more than ready to step in to the first team at any time. They may have made me No.1, but the arrival of Tim was enough to put pressure on me and keep me on my toes, which it did.

I played well enough in my first season there. The priority may have been simply to stay in the division, but I felt the team that we had was capable of *winning* that league – because in my first year we had some top class players. We had guys of the calibre of Gerry Forrest, Russell Osman, Neil 'Razor' Ruddock, Derek Statham, Jimmy Case and Glenn Cockerill, then up front we had Matthew Le Tissier, Colin Clarke and Danny Wallace, so I reckoned we were capable of winning that league by a long stretch if we could show the right level of self-belief. But some people didn't have that mindset. We'd lose at home to someone like Oxford United one week and then win away at Manchester United the next – that was the kind of team we were, but we could beat anyone on our day.

Jimmy Case in midfield was our captain and he had a notorious name at the time for being a bit of a drinker and a hardman. I used to call him 'The Quiet Assassin'. He was deaf and a bit blind too. He was a big, big name in football after all he'd done with Liverpool, winning European Cups and titles, and was recognised as the master of the long pass. He could put a 35-yard pass on a sixpence. But he also had a ruthless streak, which he disguised cleverly. If ever you needed someone to sort a problem or a troublesome player in a match then Jimmy Case was your man. He could steam in and leave someone writhing on the ground in agony, and be 10 yards away from the incident in the blink of an eye. He would kick somebody and get out of there pronto, instead of standing there arguing about it and turning it into a drama. When I went to Southampton I wrongly had him marked as someone with a foul temper and a bit of a bad reputation for kicking people, but to my surprise I found him a complete gentleman. Jimmy rarely said a word and I never saw him drunk. I remember seeing his caring side on the bus coming back from Old Trafford after beating Manchester United 2-0. We all piled on to the coach in high spirits, and Jimmy took the time to go round his team-mates thanking each and every one of them for their efforts. We were on the motorway and Jimmy came up and said: 'Great game, John.' Before I knew it, he had put pasta in the microwave for me, served it to up to me on a tray, got me a knife and fork and put a can of beer in my hand. This was the captain, and after all he'd done in the game, he could be forgiven for having an ego, but he was always the gentleman off the park, although not on the pitch when some loudmouth was asking for it.

Every away trip was a long trip for Southampton, and the bus would get in a real mess after those lengthy journeys on the motorway. There would be beer cans, packs of crisps and Mars bar wrappers all over the place, but not when Jim was on board – he had a touch of OCD I think, and was always making sure everything was neat and tidy. I'm a bit like that myself. Everything had to be immaculate around him and he couldn't stand seeing an empty beer can out of place. He was the best captain I ever had. On the field he used to kick people that needed kicking, fire in great shots and split defences with his passes and incredible vision. Off the field he was a class act too, always looking out for his team-mates. His eyesight was a bit iffy, but he would kick balls over the full-back for Le Tissier and Wallace to run on to with pinpoint accuracy. I asked him what his secret was, how he could hit balls inch-perfect from distance, and he would just shrug and say: 'There should be somebody there.' I said: 'What, you play by instinct?' And he replied: 'Exactly, John' (he wouldn't call me 'Budgie') with a glint in his eye. He just instinctively knew where players would be on the pitch around him. It was a special gift that very few players have.

The first year at The Dell went well – nothing spectacular, but everyone was happy enough. In my second year, being a dedicated professional I used to stay back after training most days for 30-45 minutes and take the kids for a bit of shooting practice and some crossing. I would always pick a centre-forward so he could challenge me and I could work on my cross-balls under pressure. I used to say to whoever I had picked: 'For goodness sake, give it to me, because I'm going to give it to you, so don't hold back.'

As I was put through my paces – coming out for crosses – there was one young lad I used to knee in the kidneys, in the ribs, in the lungs, and I could hear him gasping for breath. I did it to help toughen him up and to work on my own protection methods. I expected him to cry 'enough', but he kept coming back for more. I had played with Andy Gray – the master of getting his elbows up and giving goalkeepers as good as he got – so this kid used to always come and ask me questions about how Andy Gray used to jump, how he would beat goalkeepers and central defenders to the ball in the air. Andy was obviously a big hero and inspiration to him, and I was still in constant touch with my old Villa and Wolves team-mate, so he didn't hesitate to tap in to my first-hand knowledge. This kid had great big thighs, but no real upper body muscle, so some afternoons when I was in the gym at The Dell I would give him tips to help make him tougher and bigger. He needed toughening up, no doubt about it, but he was eager to learn. There was an incident in training during the five-a-side drills we used to have. There was a through ball, 50-50 with me and the kid, and as I dived to get the ball he pulled out of the challenge and jumped over the top of me. I got to my feet and threw the ball at him smack-bang on the back of the head.

I screamed at him: 'Are you going to play like a woman all your life?'

He just stared at me, frozen to the spot, before I explained to him: 'That's exactly what the keeper wants you to do – pull out of the challenge. You are allowed to block-tackle in his chest.' I went on: 'Don't be dirty, but don't jump over me again or I'll hit you.'

He was a bit frightened because he was only a 16-year-old lad. Seven or eight years later, that incident came back to bite me on the arse. I was playing for Falkirk and we were playing a friendly against Blackburn Rovers, but as I dived at the feet of their forward…BANG, my lights went out. I lost a couple of teeth and got a couple of stitches in a face wound, and as I looked up after the incident the young fella from all those years before on the Southampton training ground was standing there, protesting: 'YOU told me to do it! You told me not to hold back!' You know who the boy was…Alan Shearer! I nurtured him and coaxed a bit more out of him back then when he was 16, and as everyone knows he went on to have a magnificent career.

To be honest, Alan Shearer had limited skill. He may not have been technically the greatest player in the world, but my God that kid wanted it so bad to be a successful footballer. At one stage, Southampton nearly released him, but he would work and work, always eager to learn and improve his game.

He was only 17 when Chris Nicholl called him up to play in the first team. Alan used to babysit Thomas and Katie – my children – for a fiver a night when me and Janet would go out for our dinner. He became a friend and I had so much admiration for his attitude on the pitch and training ground. It was no surprise that he got called up by Chris at such a young age, because his dedication was unbelievable. He was like me in that respect – not the best, but he tried and tried and put as much as he humanly could into the game. Young Shearer made his full debut against Arsenal on 9 April, 1988 – a daunting prospect for any kid because in those days Tony Adams and Martin Keown formed the rock of the Arsenal defence.

I went over to him in the dressing room before the game and said to him: 'It's only Arsenal, we can beat these!' And he was in front of me as we went down the tunnel so again I put my hands on his shoulders and said to him: 'C'mon son, you can do it, you've done all that training, you've go nothing to worry about.' I don't know if my words had any bearing, but he was certainly not overawed. He went out onto the field and scored with practically his first kick. He then scored again with a great typical Shearer diving header. His forte in his early these days was running on to a ball pinged between the centre-half and full-back. He would chase paper on a windy day, he was so keen! Ten minutes before the end he completed his hat-trick – against Arsenal; what a debut! We won that game 4-2, but Chris rested him for the next game, just to protect him a bit. Chris looked after him very well in the early days because he could have been burnt out if he wasn't handled carefully, or the success could have gone to his head. But Chris Nicholl did an absolutely brilliant job in keeping young Shearer's feet on the ground. I've always considered him a good friend and we kept in touch.

Another unbelievable incident that occurred at Southampton, which would come back to haunt me later in my career at Newcastle, was the time we played Tottenham Hotspur at The Dell in the league. They had all the big stars at that time, including Ossie Ardiles and Ricky Villa, who had been World Cup winners with Argentina. It was a night game, but the floodlights at The Dell weren't the best because they sat on top of the stand. I think it affected their keeper, Bobby Mimms, because he was having a bit of a nightmare. We went 1-0 in front when Glenn Cockerill scored with a deflection that went up in the air and over Mimmsy, who probably should have had it.

It was a real knife-edge game, and with us hanging on at 1-0 they got a corner in the last minute. Before they could take it, I got to the ball first and tried to waste a few precious seconds. Little Ossie came sprinting over to me, screaming: 'Give me ball, give me ball!' and trying to prise it out of my grasp. I just said to him: 'In one minute you can have the ball and let your kids play with it for all I care, just not yet.' I handed it over, slow as I could, and as he turned round I gave him a little push. It was the slightest of nudges but he went down theatrically to the ground, holding his face and whining. 'Referee, referee, he elbow me, ELBOW!' I was furious that he was trying to get me sent off. I leaned over him and shouted at him to get up and get on with taking the corner.

When the corner was eventually taken, Ossie was to find out that I had a beautiful little trick up my sleeve, purely in the interests of self-preservation. Because people used to try to stand on me at corners all the time, I used to retaliate by breaking the metatarsal bone in the top of their foot. I used to work on my back studs – filing them down so they were like arrowheads. When the officials came into the dressing room before a game, nine times out of 10 they only had time to quickly run their fingers over the front studs and do the quickest of safety checks on boots. But the back studs on mine were like bullets because I'd filed them down. The reason was simple – when people came up to me at a corner and tried to bully and intimidate me, or to stop me getting to the ball first, I'd take matters into my own hands. I wasn't stupid about it. I'd have a look at the referee first, then the linesman, and if they were both looking the other way then I'd seize the moment. I'd bring my left or right boot down on the striker's metatarsal – BANG! It sounds cruel and dirty, but it was kick or be kicked, because the centre-forward would do it to you first if you showed even the slightest weakness. It was a necessary evil. When Spurs eventually took their last-minute corner that night, Ossie tried to get in a sneaky stamp, trying to tread on my feet. There was only one thing for it – I gave him the old two-studs combination on the metatarsal, and he went down in absolute agony. Our defence cleared the ball upfield and we had won the game.

When the final whistle went I did my usual ritual and ran to the Southampton fans to applaud the crowd at the top end of the ground. But as I was clapping them I heard this shrill voice in my ear behind me, hissing: 'You ANIMAL!' It was an irate Ossie, and he was behind me all the way as I went down the tunnel. At Southampton there was a flight of 10 stairs on the way to the dressing rooms, and as I started to near them I could still hear Ossie going crackers behind me. I saw that Terry Venables, who was in charge of Tottenham and a man I had the greatest of respect for, was nearby and I warned him: 'Terry, get him away from me, you know what I'm like and what I'll do to him.' But as I got to the top of the stairs Ossie sneaked up behind me on my blind side and pushed me. I started to stumble down the stairs, but managed to stop myself after I'd slid down three or four of the steps. I tried to control my temper, but he was still gobbing off at me, so I smacked him. I told Terry to take him out of my sight and away to the dressing room or I'd break his neck. Britain had just been at war with Argentina over the Falklands, and I lost it at that stage, shouting: 'We've just beat you in the Falklands, now I've just beaten you here, now fuck off!' My head had completely gone. I shouldn't have said it, but he'd pushed me way too far.

After the game, a complaint was filed by Tottenham Hotspur about my behaviour after the game. It was kept between the clubs, and the FA were not involved, but it annoyed me that it was all being put on me and that it was being suggested that Ossie Ardiles was blameless in the whole incident. I was later summoned to the manager's office and when I told Chris that he had pushed me down the stairs, and that I was only trying to mind my own business, he accepted that. That was the end of the matter...or so I thought. My clash with Ossie would resurface later in my career – in spectacular fashion.

CHAPTER 16

HOWAY THE LAD

*'Losing in the play-offs to Sunderland was one of my
most heartbreaking moments in football.'*

I had three fantastic years at Southampton, but it wasn't the
biggest of clubs, and to me it seemed football would never
come first in the city. That irked me a bit, because I like cities that
are as passionate about their football as they can possibly be.
After three years with Southampton, I started to hear rumours
that Newcastle United were interested in signing me. Coming
from that part of the world I knew what size of club it was and
what football meant to the people there. Newcastle were in the
Second Division at the time, which would mean taking a step
down a division again, but that didn't bother me because I knew
with my track record of helping to get teams up, we had a great
chance of getting promoted. At first it was just newspaper talk
and I didn't hear anything further. I kept waiting and waiting for
a phone call, and all the while Chris – justifiably – was warning
me that unless I signed a new contract at Southampton he
couldn't play me and he'd play Timmy instead.

I was on tenterhooks and had a strong gut feeling the call

would come from Newcastle. It eventually came through an agent called Steve Wicks, who had been my centre-half at QPR, and he knew the Newcastle manager Jim Smith very well. He confirmed that Newcastle wanted me, so I jumped into my Porsche and drove up there on the Sunday. By that time Thomas had taken up ice hockey, and because the kids had such a happy life down in Southampton, I had to make sure that they wouldn't miss out on the things they enjoyed if we moved north. I chose Durham as the ideal place to live, because they had the big ice hockey team of the day and I wanted to encourage Thomas. I didn't want to live in Newcastle because it's a big, sprawling, industrial city, and I wanted to live somewhere neutral. I met Jim Smith to talk over the potential move, but to be honest he didn't need to sell the club to me – I could see for myself what a huge club Newcastle United were and I didn't hesitate for a second to sign. Everything I asked for I got, and I saw the move to Newcastle as a great opportunity for me, because I was 38 years old. I regarded them almost as my hometown club, because although I was brought up in Workington in the north-west, Newcastle was only about 60 miles away, and the club had a huge following in the surrounding area.

It was a great feeling to go to Newcastle; there was a vibe about the place that convinced me that this was one move that was meant to be. Jim Smith was an excellent manager, and like me he was a bit of an eccentric. He was part of the reason the move was so attractive to me. He shouted a lot, but I was now at the age where I could take it when it was dished out. When I had been at Villa and Ron Saunders was giving me earache, I could be a bit of a shrinking violet and I couldn't take being shouted and screamed at. But by this stage of my career, managers could say pretty much whatever they wanted because I had been through the mill and played hundreds of games, so it was easy to take – water off a duck's back.

My first season went unbelievably well and off the pitch everything was rosy too. I had managed to find a lovely house in Durham – a former monastery – although I had lost £75,000 on my house in Southampton, having paid £300,000. On the pitch, we had a team full of characters and good professionals – including Micky 'The Mighty' Quinn and Roy Aitken, the Scottish international, who I quickly became very good friends with. Roy and I were the non-drinkers of the team and wouldn't be seen in the nightclubs, so we bonded right away. I think a lot of people saw me and my eccentricities and immediately thought I must be a bit of a drinker because I was outgoing and liked a laugh, but that was never me. Because of my antics, people thought I must be a wild man and a big bevvy merchant, but they were a millions miles away from the truth because I was totally dedicated to my football. I'd be in bed early if I was playing, because matches and making the most out my career were what mattered to me more than anything. You do hear of a lot of players from that era who thought the best way for a team to function was to play together and drink together, but Roy Aitken and I were proof that you didn't have to drink to be respected and be part of the team.

Roy was Captain Fantastic for us. He was a hard boy and he kept the team running. He was a terrific professional. The first year I had at Newcastle was great, we were fighting for promotion all the way and I got voted player of the season after a string of solid performances. As we neared the end of the season, we had a great chance to go up. We played Middlesbrough, and if we had won we would have got promoted to the First Division. Boro were in a bad way at that time. Their existence was under threat and they had to win to stay up and have any hope of keeping the bank manager at bay. We should have wanted a win in that game as much as they did, but for some reason they were more fired up than us on the day and they beat us 4-1 at Ayresome Park, which was a grim place to play. My memories of Ayresome Park are particularly unpleasant, as it was the one ground where fans would throw everything at you, including piss! I'm not joking; when you went to ask for the ball back from the crowd for a goal kick they would chuck plastic cups full of piss on you and saturate you.

The defeat against Boro put us into play-offs in May 1990 and as fate would have it, we had to play Sunderland – our greatest rivals. You hear all about Celtic v Rangers, Manchester United v City and Liverpool v Man Utd, but this rivalry was every bit as fierce. It's a huge game up there in the north east – Geordies v Mackems – and to be up against Sunderland in the play-offs was one of the biggest games ever between the teams.

We went to their old ground, Roker Park, on the Saturday for the first leg and it was packed. I had one of my best games in a Newcastle shirt, and with the score at 0-0 in the 90th minute they won a penalty. I'd seen the Sunderland left-back Paul Hardyman take penalties before, because when I wasn't playing I used to watch a lot of games during the week and I'd seen him stick one to the keeper's right against Torquay. I had a funny feeling he was going to put it the same way, and he did. I leapt low to my right and made a decent stop. The Newcastle fans went mad, but the lights went out for me – Hardyman's frustration boiled over and after missing the penalty, he followed up by kicking me right in the face as I lay on the ground clutching the ball. All the Newcastle lads went crazy, and it turned into a free for all, while I lay oblivious to the battle going on around me as I stayed down on the turf. Hardyman was sent off for booting me in the head, denying me any chance of revenge, and everything seemed stacked in Newcastle's favour to beat them in the return leg.

After my penalty save I thought to myself that it was all fated – I was completely convinced we were going to win the second leg at St James' Park. It was a funny situation, because whoever won would be going up. Swindon Town were about to be punished for alleged financial irregularities, so whoever got to the final at Wembley – Newcastle or Sunderland – would automatically be promoted, regardless of their result against Swindon, as they were heading for the trapdoor anyway.

The atmosphere was frenzied for the return leg, but my pre-match vibes that Newcastle were going to finish the job were proved sadly wrong. Eric Gates and Marco Gabbiadini scored for Sunderland and they beat us 2-0 at St James' Park – it was devastating. It wasn't a nice game to play in, and I'm not just saying that because we lost. I love derbies, but there was just too much at stake for both sides and there was an ugly atmosphere. The fans' frustration boiled over, and a pitch invasion after the second goal held the game up for half an hour. Losing that game was definitely one of the most heartbreaking moments for me in football, especially after I had stopped that penalty in the first leg from Hardyman. But, the way I look at it, everything happens for a reason. If we'd gone up that season Newcastle might not have enjoyed the revival they experienced under Kevin Keegan four or five years later, and seen their ground transformed into the magnificent stadium it is today. I later ended up working for the club for 12 years as a player and a coach so I was well placed to judge a few years down the line. In my opinion, if they had gone up back in 1990, Newcastle would have remained the yo-yo side that they always had been. We would have gone up in 1990 and straight back down again – we weren't well enough equipped for a sustained run in the top flight at that time. It all changed when Sir John Hall bought Newcastle and brought Kevin Keegan in. They bought guys like Les Ferdinand, Philippe Albert, Alan Shearer, Robert Lee – all unbelievable players – but I honestly think none of that would have happened had we gone up in 1990.

The play-off disaster aside, I really enjoyed my first season at Newcastle, and I was playing out of my skin at 39 years old. Sadly, Jim Smith carried the can for failing to get us up and he got the sack towards the end of the following season. There were three or four games left of the season, and as we sat in the training ground it was announced that the new manager was being brought to meet us. Nobody knew who it was, it was all hush-hush.

We were all sitting there in the dressing room speculating who it might be, when the chairman Gordon McKeag came in and announced with great gusto: 'I want to introduce to you the new manager of Newcastle United Football Club...'

The door opened and in walked my old sparring partner, Osvaldo Ardiles. The incident at The Dell, where I had clocked him for pushing me down the stairs, immediately invaded my thoughts. My mind was racing and I honestly managed to convince myself that he wouldn't remember – it was ancient history and water under the bridge as far as I was concerned.

He started going round the dressing room smiling and shaking hands with the players, and when he arrived in front of me, the chairman – blissfully ignorant of the history we shared – said: 'And this is John Burridge, our star goalkeeper...'. I extended my hand for him to shake, but he totally blanked me and walked on to the next player.

'This isn't good,' I thought to myself, and went home for a sleepless night. I trained the next day, and began to think it would all just be a storm in a teacup. The team were due to play West Ham at the weekend, then Charlton Athletic the following Tuesday in two back-to-back away games, so the plan was for the squad to stay down in London for the duration of the two matches. The day before we were due to head south, I was in my car when Janet phoned to say she'd just seen the local paper and it was reporting that I'd been dropped. 'No chance,' I thought, as we'd just won 2-0 in our last game and I'd saved a penalty. But when I got to the training ground my kit wasn't in its normal place in the first-team dressing room. I asked the kit man where it was and he sheepishly told me that the manager had ordered him to put it in the reserves' dressing room. Ardiles hadn't even had the guts to tell me, and instead word was passed down through the ranks that he wanted me to train with the reserves.

I still couldn't believe it. I thought he was just trying to scare me, so when the team bus was about to leave for London I still turned up in my suit and club tie, ready to head down with the rest of the lads. It was when I read the team-sheet and saw my name wasn't on it I knew it was no joke. I got into my car, totally disappointed, my thoughts all over the place as I tried to make some sense of it all. With Osvaldo down in London with the team, the earliest chance I would get to speak to him face to face would be the Wednesday. So I bided my time till the Wednesday, then headed in to St James' Park for a showdown. As I was standing in reception, ready to have my say, the secretary Russell Cushing came down and said: 'Sorry John, the boss wants you out of here. He doesn't want you on the training ground; he doesn't want to see your face in the club again.'

BUDGIE

I had two years left on my contract so it was a lot to take in. It was obvious that he harboured grudges big time. I couldn't believe that he didn't have the guts to tell me himself.

CHAPTER 17
HIB, HIB HOORAY

*'A forward booted me right in the face and burst my
nose. I could just hear him growling "Welcome tae
Scotland, ya Sassenach".'*

My treatment at the hands of Ossie Ardiles at Newcastle was
difficult to take at the time, but it proved to be career-
changing – and for the better. This cloud really did have a silver
lining. When Ardiles was appointed and froze me out, it was near
the end of the season and there were only four or five games left.
I had won the player of the year award that year and even though
it was traditionally presented to the winner on the pitch at the last
home game of the season, Ardiles wouldn't let me have it. Micky
Quinn and I were the best sellers at the time or merchandise in the
Newcastle club shop, but when I popped in all the signed pictures
of me had been taken off the shelves, and so had the No.1 jerseys.
He was trying to obliterate every last trace of me from Newcastle,
and I thought he must really have hated me.

I didn't even get picked for the reserves, so I just trained and
saw the season out. In the summertime I was contemplating my
future and what to do next. My old club, Blackpool, who were
in the Third Division, came in for me, which would have been a
nice move, and Hartlepool also made an offer, which would have

allowed me to stay at home in Durham. Falkirk, who were managed by Jim Jefferies, had also been alerted that I was available, and I played a pre-season game for them with a view to going there. But as I was pondering those possibilities I got a call from Hibernian one night. Their manager Alex Miller rang me up and said: 'Do you fancy trying something different – the Scottish Premier League? Come up and see me, and have a look for yourself.'

This was all happening a week before pre-season training was about to start, and there was no time to waste. I got on the train from Durham, and was first of all surprised at how short the journey was – an hour and 20 minutes. The journey up was scenic, and I was already getting good vibes. When you get off the train at the Waverley Station, Edinburgh is one of the most impressive cities you have ever seen in your life – as you come up the ramp from the station you see the big castle on your left and Princes Street on your right. I liked the cobbled streets and I thought to myself this is a nice place to be. I took a taxi down to the Hibs ground, Easter Road, which was a nice little stadium – and I got a feel for what Scottish football is all about.

When I met Alex Miller, he explained to me: 'We've sold Andy Goram to Glasgow Rangers for a million pounds, and we've only got a couple of kids, Chris Reid and Jason Gardiner, as keepers and I don't know if they are ready yet for playing week-in, week-out in the Premier League.' I was impressed by the city and the club, and I decided I would give it a go. We came to an agreement on my salary – it wasn't a lot in terms of a weekly wage, but I was 39 and there was a good signing-on fee, so we shook hands on the deal.

What I didn't realise when I signed was the trouble Hibs had been in at that time. I didn't know anything about Scottish football as all my attention had been on English football, and apart from looking at Aberdeen's results from time to time when Ian Porterfield was manager, I hadn't paid much attention to the Scottish Premier League.

I had to report for pre-season training a few days later, so I caught the train up and headed down to their training ground at Wardie where I would meet up with my new team-mates. To say it was a shock doesn't do it justice – it was the worst training ground I'd ever seen in my life. It was basically a public park. You got changed inside a hut and the showers didn't work properly. At clubs like Aston Villa and Newcastle, I had been used to purpose-built training grounds where you would be well looked after. I was used to being given breakfast and a cup of tea and having people fussing around you. But at Hibs, we had a dive of a training ground, and the players started turning up looking down in the dumps.

I then started hearing stories that there was no money in the club, that they'd nearly gone bankrupt, and that a fella called Wallace Mercer, the chairman of their rivals Hearts, had tried to put them out of business to make Edinburgh a one-club city. I heard that people had been threatening to kill him or shoot him because of what he was trying to do to Hibs. I thought to myself: 'What have you let yourself in for here, Budgie?'

We started training and it was all very downbeat. I took that for three or four days then said to myself: 'I've got to do something to lift this place'. I was reading the Edinburgh evening papers and all the talk was how the players were unsure of their futures. The season before I arrived, 1990/91, Hibs came close to being relegated as they'd finished ninth of the 10 teams. The league was reconstructed to make it a bigger 12-team league, and while they would have stayed up anyway as only one team went down, everyone knew Hibs had beaten the drop by the skin of their teeth.

I didn't know any of that when I signed. I hadn't done my homework if I'm being honest, and all the emphasis was on keeping away from relegation; that was the chat – from the manager as well – because they had fought a relegation dogfight the year before and it was still preying on their minds. It was a terrible atmosphere and I thought: 'C'mon Budgie, you have to work your magic here,' so I started the old Budgie antics around the dressing room, making people laugh and lifting their spirits. I remember one morning I let the rest of the lads go out before me, telling them I'd be out once I'd put some tape on my fingers. They were all out on the pitch, kicking a ball about, when I ran out to join them totally starkers – apart from my goalie gloves!

We played four or five pre-season games against part-timers up in the north of Scotland. We didn't do very well – we were hopeless in fact, drawing or losing against a bunch of amateurs. I knew we had to start winning and quick. I knew if we couldn't beat Highland League teams then we could be heading for trouble.

I looked at the team and we weren't bad – we had some good players, we just had a problem with motivation and belief. So I started having a laugh and a joke around the place and all of a sudden it was a bit more joyful and we started to get rid of the bad feeling that had been created by Wallace Mercer and his attempted takeover. But the only way you can truly get rid of that feeling is by winning football matches. It was as simple as that.

We played St Mirren in the first game of the season on home turf, and I knew that a win was vital, because a defeat could sap morale and set the tone for a long, hard season. The Scottish Premier League was of a much better standard than I thought it would be. I mistakenly thought it might be Third

Division standard, but when we kicked off I soon knew I'd misjudged it. In the first 20 minutes we were awful, just far too nervous and inferior in our minds because we didn't have the winning mentality. I remember a cross came over and someone gave me a right good clatter and I dropped it. I gathered it at the second attempt, but the forward booted me in the face. My nose was all bleeding, and I could just hear a voice in a broad Scottish accent growling: 'Welcome tae Scotland, ya fuckin' Sassenach.' I was playing against my pal from Newcastle, Roy Aitken, who had moved to St Mirren because he couldn't get along with Ossie either, and I knew he was an out-and-out winner and would have them fired up. But whatever they threw at us, we threw back. We settled down and started to play out of our skins; we won it 4-1, and I was delighted with my own performance too. I ran to the fans, on a crest of a wave, and they seemed to take to me right away as I bowed before them and threw my gloves into the crowd.

We then won our second game, against St Johnstone, so we were off to as great start, and kept up the good work by going the first 10 league games unbeaten. The lads started believing, and you could see them visibly growing in confidence. They were enjoying their football again. I was playing as well as I had done in my career and I made the crowd laugh with my gymnastics. I was playing up to them, putting the smiles back on their faces, and it was a completely different atmosphere. A local millionaire called Tom Farmer, who had made his fortune from the Kwik-Fit garage chain, had come in and put an awful lot of money in to stabilise the club, and I think he had helped pay for Keith Wright, who we had signed from Dundee for half-a-million. Tom had bought the club first and foremost to stop Wallace Mercer shutting it down, but to his delight we had made an unbelievable start to the season.

I had a system of defending that Terry Venables had shown me at Crystal Palace which I took with me to any club I was at – it was like shoving the opposition down a funnel. I was basically coaching the defence while I was on the pitch. Alex Miller used to watch me doing this at training with players like Murdo MacLeod and my full-backs Graham Mitchell and Willie Miller, and I noticed that he used that same method a few years later when he was Scotland assistant manager to Craig Brown. The gist of the system was that we wouldn't let teams play down the outside on the wings; everything would get pushed down the middle where they would run into players like Pat McGinlay or Brian Hamilton, who could both tackle. It was simple, but effective. If opponents beat me once or twice a season from 25 yards down the middle then I could accept that, but if you allow teams to keep getting crosses in from wide areas then they are going to hurt you and you will concede a lot of goals.

I was coaching this method and we started to adapt to this new system comfortably. You could see the central defenders Tommy McIntyre and 'Geebsy', Gordon Hunter, believing in themselves and getting stronger. Gordon wasn't the tallest lad in the world, but he was a brilliant tackler and he was quick. Tommy was strong and excellent in the air, but to begin with he was a little bit soft and timid. He had everything needed to become a fantastic centre-back. I told him he was good enough to be an international, but first I had to get him to stop being so negative in his thinking. Everything was going well and Alex Miller seemed happy enough to let me get on with it and use this system because we were winning football matches and keeping clean sheets, with Mickey Weir and Keith Wright banging in the goals at the other end. From being a skint club that was on the verge of going bankrupt, we were riding high in the league and enjoying a great season.

CHAPTER 18

HAMPDEN HERO

*'I had never seen anything like the scenes in
Edinburgh that night.'*

The League Cup, or Skol Cup as it was known then, comes
thick and fast in Scotland and back in those days it would
be all over and done with by the end of October. It was a good
format, and it captured the public's imagination because you'd
be playing every week. I hadn't being paying too much attention
to cup runs because my main concern was to keep Hibernian in
the Premier League after all the pre-season talk about relegation.
But we beat Stirling Albion, then Kilmarnock, then Ayr United in
the quarter-finals – all away from home – and before we knew it
we'd made it into the semi-finals by September.

We got drawn out of the hat to play Glasgow Rangers at
Hampden Park and obviously they were going to be big favourites
to win that game. It was the height of the Graeme Souness era and
their team was packed full of internationals. They had one
hundred times the budget Hibs had, and they always fielded their
strongest team in the League Cup. It was the first time I had played
against them, and the first time I had been able to play against

Andy Goram – who had been something of a Hibs hero and the man I'd been bought to replace. I had heard stories about Andy Goram from the lads that I couldn't believe. While I was Mr Dedication, I heard how they used to have to pour coffee down his throat or give him a hot bath to get him fit enough to play because he had been drinking like a fish before games. They said he would be in some terrible states, but then would go out and play brilliantly. That was the complete opposite to me. I would be in bright and early, doing my warm-up routine and preparing for games, so I was sick of hearing about Goram and what a wonderful keeper he'd been. I would ask them: 'If he was so great, how did you nearly get relegated last year?'

It was my first time playing at Hampden. All the lads were buzzing though and the green end of Edinburgh was on fire, but Alex Miller took a bit of geeing up. I've come across a lot of pessimists in my life, but Alex Miller was *the* biggest pessimist I have ever seen. At the start of the season I had to battle the team's collective depression, but I constantly had to battle the manager's depression as well. He used to give long-winded team talks about how good Partick Thistle or St Mirren were. He would tell us that Chic Charnley was going to belt one in from 25 yards, that he was going to break everyone's legs, that he needed to be watched – going on and on and on about this team. I eventually snapped and said: 'For God's sake boss, it's Saint fucking Mirren not Saint Peter we're dealing with! I've played about 700 top-league games and you're trying to make me scared of St Soddin' Mirren!' All the lads were giggling away in the dressing room as they saw Miller's serious face develop into an even darker frown, but I had the bit between the teeth and I went on: 'Don't stand there telling us what they are going to do to us, tell us what we are going to do to THEM!'

I wanted him to be optimistic and to have them worrying

about us. But before the Rangers game, he started it all again, bigging them up during the team talk in the hotel. He had played for them in the 1970s and obviously was in awe of them a bit. He was raving about how good they all were – Ally McCoist, Pieter Huistra, Mark Hateley, John Brown and Mo Johnston. He said to me: 'Budgie, see Hateley – be careful, he's going to mince you in the first few minutes. He does it to all goalkeepers; he hammers you, and smashes into you with his elbows.' I couldn't believe what I was hearing and I said back to him: 'Young Mark? His old dad [Tony] might have tried to do it to me when I was 16 at Workington, and he was playing for Notts County, but this fucker isn't going to do it to me.' The lads were falling about laughing. For good measure, I added: 'I'll put *him* in the hospital. Talk about us, not about them.'

He didn't know what to say, he was gobsmacked.

When we got to Hampden, I was in the dressing room before the game telling jokes and playing pranks, putting people's stockings in the showers, that kind of thing, when Alex Miller came over and told me to be serious. Now, anyone will tell you I am deadly serious when a game starts, but if you're helping to make people laugh in the dressing room it takes pressure off the game. If you got out there with a smile on your face, you play better.

Miller asked me again: 'Are you being serious, Budgie?' That rattled me a bit and I said: 'I'll show you how serious I am.' So when we got into the Hampden tunnel, where both of the teams were lining up and preparing to be led out, I spotted Hateley and gave it to him with both barrels. I shouted at him: 'Hey Hateley, I'm going to break your back if you come in my six-yard box, you big fairy!' I saw McCoist trying not to laugh, so I turned my guns on him. 'I dunno what you're laughing at, McCoist. You were a failure at Sunderland and you couldn't cut it, son. You've had to come back to Scotland and beg for a game!' Murdo MacLeod, who was the captain and player-manager, was getting a bit concerned at all the shouting and swearing and asked me what I was doing winding them up before a game, but there was no way anyone was going to stop me having my say and I continued, addressing the whole Rangers team this time (at least any of them that would look me in the eye). 'The whole lot of you are fucking rubbish,' I said. 'You play in a chewing gum league. If you want to play in a big league, come down south and prove yourselves down there!'

All the lads were laughing their heads off. I was ready to take on the whole Rangers team if they wanted a fight, I was so pumped up. I had my fists clenched and I just wanted to get out there. After the game started, in front of a full house at Hampden, I was really enjoying the occasion, and pulled off two or three great saves in the first half. I got a sharp reminder just how hard I would have to work to maintain my concentration when I made one silly mistake and dropped a cross. To my horror I saw that the ball was about to fall to Hateley – it would have been a major embarrassment for me if he'd scored after all my mouthing off – but big Tommy McIntyre pulled me out of a sticky situation by kicking it clear.

We were more than holding our own against Rangers, and we made the breakthrough just before half-time when Andy Goram mis-punched a ball to Mickey Weir on the right, who crossed it back into the box for our centre-forward Keith Wright to score with a header. I came out for everything in the second half as we battled to hold on to our one-goal lead. They were throwing men forward and I made one of the best saves of my life.

Ian Durrant hit a perfect shot, which I touched on to the

post, and as it came back to Ally McCoist, he hit it full pelt from seven or eight yards out. I got across the goal like lightning and managed to catch it, and I could hear him grumbling: 'What a fucking save.' It was our night; we had beaten a star-studded Rangers team and were heading into the final against Dunfermline on the crest of a wave.

We were big favourites to win the game, and there was an enormous Hibs crowd at Hampden expecting nothing other than victory. They felt it was fated – that they were going to win their first major trophy since 1972, and do so just over a year since they were nearly wiped off the planet by Wallace Mercer. After a tense, goalless first half, little Mickey Weir got bundled over for a penalty and big Tommy McIntyre kept his cool to put us one-ahead from the spot. When Keith Wright added a second, you could sense the emotion pouring out from the fans. We'd done it!

As *The Scotsman* newspaper reported the following day: 'Hibs' journey back from two years of abject misery was completed yesterday when the Skol Cup was won by goals from Tommy McIntyre and Keith Wright. It was Hibs' first trophy since winning the League Cup 19 years ago, and signals the return of the club to what they have has always perceived to be their rightful place at the forefront of the domestic game.'

Murdo MacLeod went up the Hampden steps to lift the trophy, and then it was time to go and properly celebrate with our fans. There were around 40,000 of them in Glasgow that day and they were demanding a lap of honour. I lifted Alex Miller up on my shoulders and said: 'C'mon, let's go.' The time for grudges was over. He was reluctant to join us for the lap of honour, but I picked him up and carried him round the pitch and made him look a hero. I told him he was the boss and he deserved a big share of the credit – which he did.

We went back to the hotel and had a good knees-up. I had won cups before, with Aston Villa and Blackpool, and a title with Crystal Palace where we had ridden through the streets of Croydon on an open-top bus, but I had never seen anything like the scenes in Edinburgh that night. As we returned from Glasgow to the outskirts of the city, we switched from the team coach to an open-top bus. I had never seen anything quite like it – for mile upon mile there were huge crowds of well-wishers lining the streets.

The whole of Edinburgh came out – even as we drove through the Hearts end of town it was packed – and it took us about three hours to get to Easter Road, where there was a full stadium waiting for us. The highlight for me was coming along Princes Street, where the crowds were 20 deep. All of the statues had been dressed up in green flags and green hats, and people had climbed up on top of them to give us a wave. Everyone was so happy Hibs had done well that season. Back at the stadium was an amazing experience too, and we went out on to the pitch to do another lap of honour. I climbed up on to the fence with the trophy and shook as many of the supporters' hands as I could – it was a wonderful feeling.

We were taken up the Royal Mile to the City Chambers to meet the Lord Provost and all the local dignitaries and receive more accolades. All the boys were in the mood for a massive party, but although I enjoyed every minute, I was no night owl, and I was content just to go back for a good night's sleep at the hotel with Janet.

The League Cup was the crowning glory of a marvellous season, considering all the doom and gloom that had been surrounding the place before a ball had been kicked. By winning the cup, we had automatically qualified for Europe; we'd also done really well in the league, finishing fourth, and got to the quarter-finals of the Scottish Cup too, so it was Hibs' best season in 20-odd years.

Playing for Hibs in Europe was great. We got a plum draw out of the hat – Anderlecht, who were on the biggest clubs around at that time and could boast a side full of internationals. There was an electrifying atmosphere at Easter Road and we should have beaten them. The German referee had a nightmare. We had got an early goal from Dave Beaumont, then he gave a penalty against me just before half-time. He said I had brought down their player Bruno Versavel, but I won the ball clean as a whistle, and was doubly annoyed when they buried the penalty. The Dutch international Peter van Vossen put them 2-1 up, and then the referee continued his horror show by sending off wee Mickey Weir, but we showed tremendous spirit and Pat McGinlay grabbed a late equaliser to give us a bit of hope for the second leg in Brussels.

The scenes in Belgium were nothing short of amazing. There were 3,000 Hibs fans over there and they sang their hearts out for the whole 90 minutes. We got off to a nightmare start when Anderlecht scored in the first five minutes, but Darren Jackson soon equalised and we gave them a torrid time. We just couldn't get that killer second, and their fans actually applauded us off the pitch and booed their own players. We'd gone out on away goals, and with our heads held high, and the fans stayed in the stadium for an hour to cheer us. Every time we started to head towards the dressing room, they would demand one more bow, and I was – as usual – at the front.

CHAPTER 19
MANAGEMENT ISSUES

*'The simmering bad blood between me and Alex
Miller boiled over during a game at Airdrie, when we
came to blows.'*

On the back of all Hibs' success, Alex Miller had just been given a fat new contract by the chairman Douglas Cromb and a fancy BMW, and while I didn't begrudge him that I felt it was my turn. Alex and I didn't see eye to eye very much, and my pitch for a new deal was to bring the underlying tension to a head. I think he resented me, because although he was trying to be the boss, he knew I had the dressing room. None of the players liked him and they were a little bit frightened of him because he was a bit of a shouter, but at this stage of my career I wasn't afraid of him, and it ended up a war of attrition between us as to who was going to be the boss.

When I started my contract talks, Miller already had his new deal signed and sealed. He had been given his rightful share of the credit for a good season, but I felt I was being given no recognition for the part I had played in lifting the lads. His words at the start of the season had been all about beating relegation, but I had aimed higher than that. The club had brought in an

awful lot of money as we'd got into the Uefa Cup, won the
League Cup and done well in the league.

When I first came to Hibs I was paying £20 out of my own
pocket for my return fare from Durham to Edinburgh every
day, plus another tenner for a taxi from the station down to
the training ground and back. I eventually bought a rail season
ticket for about £450, so I could travel any time, and I also
bought myself a small motor bike, as I used to like them when
I was a kid and I thought it would be handy for zipping
around. It was just a little 150cc Yamaha and I used to park it
in the Waverley Station on the bike rack. It was perfect for me,
because when I had to queue for a taxi and head into traffic
jams I could never gauge how much time it would take me to
get down to training. But on the motorbike I was always at the
front of the queue, and I knew I could get to and from the
Waverley in less than 10 minutes. One day, however, I was
running late and it's a bugbear of mine that I don't like being
late for training. My usual routine was to get there about 45
minutes before the rest of the lads, so I could do my own
technical work. I jumped off the train and went to get my bike
so I could get down to training as quick as I possibly could. I
threw on my helmet, which I used to strap through the bike
chain so nobody could pinch it, and set off. But as I was riding
down to Wardie I became aware of a terrible smell. Then the
horrible realisation came to me – somebody had crapped in my
helmet during the night! It must have been a Hearts supporter
who had done it. As I weaved my way through the traffic, it
was seeping out the edges of my helmet and it was running
down my face – there was nothing I could do about it and it
took all my concentration to stop myself from being sick.
When I got to Wardie, I jumped into the shower and scrubbed
and scrubbed myself till there was no trace of it, and then I

scrubbed the helmet. Naturally, the lads thought it was hysterical.

The rail fares and the bike all came out of my pocket, though, and I felt after the season I had just had, I was due a raise. I went in to see Alex and told him I wanted a big increase and a £50,000 fee to sign on again, but he bluntly told me: 'You're not getting an extra penny.'

In those days, before Bosman, you couldn't just walk out on a club – they could make you play. Players were a bit like slaves in those days. Even though I was 40 years old, they could slap a million-pound transfer tag on me and stop me playing or stop my wages if they had really wanted to, and I knew Alex was well capable of doing that. It may sound like I asked for too much, but when money was involved and my contract was up I was ruthless; I had to be. I backed down a bit and said that the least the club could do was pay my season-ticket on the train, but again he said: 'No, you're playing on the same wages you did last season, not a penny more.' That was the start of my downfall at Hibs. I had been prepared to play another two or three years with them because I was very, very happy, but Alex Miller took all the goodwill out of me.

I may not have been the club captain, but I had been the heart and soul of that team the season before. After Miller's attitude to my contract, I lost my enthusiasm. Some days I didn't want to train – the first time I'd ever felt like that in my career. I hadn't lost any feeling for the club or the fans; I had just lost all respect for Alex Miller. It even got to the stage where two or three days a week I would call in ill. I just didn't want to play for Miller's Hibernian.

The new season started and my heart wasn't it, and it was affecting my form. I missed a lot of games, and would ring in with false excuses. In the past, nagging injuries like dislocated fingers, sore shins or bruised toes had never kept me out, I would just strap them up and play, but now I was using them as an excuse not to play. I would have found a new club in the Third Division in England rather than play for a team where I wasn't happy. I knew a few other clubs in Scotland had been asking about me too, but it seemed to be the case that Alex Miller was turning them down to make a point.

The simmering bad blood between me and Alex Miller boiled over during a game at Airdrie, when we came to blows. It was a foul night, lashing down with rain, and during the warm-up I had been wearing a big, waterproof, protective training top. I headed back into the dressing room to get my kit on, but two or three minutes before kick-off time I was still sitting there with my waterproof top on. Miller came up to me and barked at me: 'You've got to wear the club goalkeeper's shirt, Budgie.' It was hammering down with rain and, although he didn't know it, I was intending to wait till the last minute and put the proper goalkeeper's shirt over the top of it. But when he came over and started trying to order me around, I couldn't resist a great chance to have an argument with him, so I told him: 'No. I'm wearing this instead.' He started trying to pull the waterproof top off me so I elbowed him in the jaw.

All of a sudden he squared up to me, so I hit him and knocked him to the floor. The red mist had descended and I was on top of him, knocking hell out of him until the assistant manager Murdo MacLeod jumped on my back and clocked me over the head with a big telephone – not one of the slick little mobiles you get now, this one was like a brick. I was half dazed. Normally I wouldn't have done it, but he had been holding me against my will, and all my frustration got the better of me. The whole situation really affected the boys, because they could see I wasn't happy. I was no longer Jolly

Budgie all the time, I was Angry Budgie. It had a negative effect on the dressing room, but in my eyes it was Alex Miller's fault for not seeing me right.

Another strange incident happened during that match. To some fans and players in Scottish football back then religion was a big deal, and obviously Celtic had a big Catholic following whereas Rangers were known as the protestant club. An Airdrie player came flying into me, caught me with his studs, and shouted: 'Take that, ya Fenian bastard!' I didn't even know what a 'Fenian' was; I had never heard of the word and would have needed a dictionary to find out what it meant, so I asked him what he was talking about. When he said it meant I was a Catholic, I told him: 'I'm not one, but what's that got to with anything anyway?' To my amazement, he just said: 'Oh, okay, sorry then' and ran back up the pitch. It was totally bizarre, but Scottish football could be like that sometimes.

After the game, we got back in the dressing room and I'd played quite well, Alex tried to say well done, but I told him to stick it, telling him: 'I did it for the lads, not for you, Miller.' There was a real bad atmosphere between us, and it couldn't go on. At the end of that season Hibs released me.

I regret that I was unable to build on the success of that first season, and gone on to have a couple more happy years at Hibs, but I always felt there was a jealousy from Alex Miller as well as an inferiority complex. He was wary of me because I was a bit more popular than he was and had the confidence of the players.

One thing I do owe Alex Miller a debt of gratitude for is that he encouraged me to do my coaching badges. I started by doing my B badge, then A badge, advanced-A, and then full licence, and the Scottish Football Association paid 75 per cent of the costs. He encouraged me to start my B licence in the

MANAGEMENT ISSUES

summer of 1992, and I went to Largs and passed it. Roy Aitken was also there, and we drove each other on, and I met a lot of other good friends there. Even after I left Hibs I would head up to Largs in the summer to continue working through my coaching qualifications. Persevering with the coaching badges got me to where I am now – because if I hadn't gained those licences and qualifications, I wouldn't be doing the job that I'm doing at 58 years old. While I knew plenty about football, and understood the game, I learned more from teachers than coaches, because what I didn't know was to how to portray myself positively and speak confidently in public. I had left school with no qualifications and only knew day-to-day football. They taught me how to get my message over. All kinds of people went to Largs from all over the world. Jose Mourinho did his badges around the same time as me, but no one knew him because in those days he was just an interpreter for Bobby Robson. Everyone knew Budgie, though!

CHAPTER 20

GOALIE FOR HIRE

*'I would turn up at Newcastle on a Friday not
knowing what the weekend held for me or where I'd
be going out on loan – it was quite exciting.'*

They say that variety is the spice of life and after I'd moved
on from Hibs, things started to get really interesting. I already
had a good career under my belt, and most people might just
have considered calling it quits. After I'd been freed by
Hibernian, I must admit I did think to myself: 'What the hell am
I going to do next at the age of 42?'

I had spent two or three days agonising over what I should do
when the telephone rang, and it was Kevin Keegan, who had
been a breath of fresh air as manager of Newcastle after a
disastrous reign by Ardiles. 'Budgie? It's Kevin Keegan.' 'Hi Kev,
what's on your mind? What can I do for you?' 'Budgie, I need a
player-coach. I want you to train my goalkeepers.' And that was
that. I was back in business!

Newcastle trained in Durham, where I lived, so I said I would
come down and have a chat with him. Kevin and I had a good
talk, and he asked if I was intending to play on. The more I
thought about it, the more I realised there was no point kidding

myself that I would be happy hanging up the gloves – I still had that itch to play. 'Well, why don't you work with our goalkeepers here during the week and sit on the bench if we need you?' Kevin suggested.

At that time, Newcastle only had Pavel Srnicek and Mike Hooper as senior goalkeepers, with Steve Harper coming through the youth system, so I was third-choice goalkeeper. Kevin gave me a pretty good salary, with Premier League bonuses, so I was earning twice as much money as I had been at Hibernian and I didn't have to travel – I could walk down and walk back to training every day. It was a bloody good deal, so I didn't hesitate and signed a three-year contract with Newcastle as player-goalkeeping coach. Arthur Cox was part of Kevin's backroom team, and although I still wasn't flavour of the month with him after our incident at Derby, most of the time we were both professional enough to get on with our jobs and not let it become a day-to-day problem.

I would take the goalkeepers out at 9am and train them until 10.30, and then we would join in with the rest of the team. Kevin's training most days was kept simple – a warm-up, then straight into the five-a-sides. There was never a lot of technical stuff involved, just high-tempo five-a-sides, which the team thrived on. We had two matches on the go at the same time, so we needed four goalkeepers and that meant that I was in full-time training. I was also playing for the reserves during the week, so nobody could accuse me of taking a cushy little number – it was much harder work than I thought it would be. I would train hard on a Monday, same on a Tuesday, then nine times out of 10 I would be playing for the reserves on a Wednesday. If it was a 7pm kick-off, often I wouldn't return to Newcastle until one in the morning, then I was up for training on Thursday and training again with the keepers on a Friday.

Then on a Friday night I was away with the team, so Sunday was my only day off. The workload was very hard and it was a tough working week. I wasn't complaining though; it was well worth it. We had an excellent team and a great atmosphere, and I loved working under Kevin – I thought he was fantastic.

I was enjoying the reserve games, but there's nothing like first-team football, and I was about get my fix through a series of loan deals. I just took it week by week, and at that stage I had no idea that I would end up more than doubling the number of clubs I had played for.

I was playing head tennis with Kevin and his assistant Terry McDermott on the training ground one Friday, when Arthur came out and told me a club had been on the phone wanting me to play the next day. First it was Scarborough, then it was Lincoln, and before I knew it I was turning out for a different club every month – that's where most of my long list of clubs came from. I played for 14 clubs between 1993 and 1997.

It became common knowledge that I was available to help clubs out at short notice. Friends of Kevin or Arthur would call up and see if they could get me. Somewhere – in Scotland or in the lower leagues – a first-team keeper would break a thumb or twist an ankle, and a club would be desperate for an experienced goalkeeper at short notice. The deal was simple – I would ask for a couple of thousand pounds and for Janet and me to be put up in a hotel. We used to make a weekend of it. If Newcastle didn't want me to sit on the bench, then I was free to sign short-term loan deals elsewhere. I would take a month's loan, and the club would have to pay me for that month. I used to really enjoy the change of scenery, driving down to Scarborough, or going to Aberdeen or Falkirk to play two or three games. But I would always go back to Newcastle.

I enjoyed my time up at Aberdeen especially. I wasn't there long, but I still had a good rapport with all the fans up there from my time at Hibs, and I got to play in some big matches against old sparring partners like Hearts and Rangers. Their Dutch keeper, Theo Snelders, was injured and Willie Miller knew what I was capable of from my spell at Easter Road, so didn't have any hesitation putting me straight in goal for the game against Rangers in front of 40,000 at Ibrox. I liked Aberdeen as a city too, although it did make me think once again what might have been had I chosen to go there earlier in my career instead of signing for Southampton.

I would turn up at Newcastle on a Friday not knowing what the weekend held for me or where I'd be going out on loan – it was quite exciting. But never in my wildest dreams did I think Newcastle would let me go on loan to another Premier League team. Then one day I saw Arthur coming towards me, ready to send me on my travels again.

'What have you got for me this time, Arthur?' I asked. 'Manchester City want you to sit on the bench,' he told me. 'Andy Dibble's broken a finger.'

Francis Lee, the ex-England international, was the City chairman of the time – like Kevin, he was a big horse-racing man and was very friendly with him. That's how he'd got wind of the fact I might be free to play for them. I went to Kevin and pointed out to him: 'This is Manchester City; they're in the Premier League...the same league as us.' But he just said: 'No problem Budgie, get your arse down there.'

I was quite happy to go to Man City on loan, but from September to April I was just sitting on the bench, making up the numbers. Tony Coton was in goal and I was there as the back-up man. The way the arrangement worked, I would go down to Manchester on a Thursday night, train with City, then stay in the Copthorne Hotel. I enjoyed going to City's old Maine Road ground and putting on my strip. I think I drove them all nuts with my enthusiasm though – I couldn't keep still in the dressing room, and I got a telling-off one week for diving about in the tunnel. I had all that natural energy pent up, and no proper way of releasing it. I pity whoever had to sit next to me on the bench as I fidgeted my way through 90 minutes.

City were in big relegation trouble during that 1994/95 season and we started to fear we might go down as we were sucked into the bottom four. Meanwhile Newcastle were flying and were going for a European place, but they too started dropping points at an alarming rate towards the business end of the season. It was a bizarre feeling, being torn between the two clubs, and I wanted them both to do as well as possible. I was only at Newcastle 75 per cent of the time, but would still train like a donkey and put in every effort I could when I was on the Newcastle training ground. I was working just as hard when I went down to City and that was no mean feat for a goalie of 43. The arrangement was working well, but then in April, an awkward situation arose when Newcastle were due to play City at Maine Road. Newcastle needed every point to nail down a European place and they had come down from being 19 points clear of their nearest challengers to five. I had a strange feeling about potentially stopping Newcastle winning points, even if it was highly unlikely I'd be playing, so I thought it was only right to go and see Kevin the Monday morning before the game.

'You know that we play City this week?' I said to Kevin. 'Yeah...' 'I'll be on the bench.' 'Yeah...' 'Funny things happen in football, Kevin, what if I have to play?' 'Budgie,' he said, 'it's a one-in-a-hundred chance that you'll come on and play.' I replied: 'If you want, I'll ask them to put a young boy on the

bench because it would be terrible if I had to play.' But Kevin
said: 'It's not a problem with me, Budgie.'

I trained all week with Newcastle and I went back to see him
again on the Thursday and asked if he was sure he was okay
with me playing. I think I was getting on his nerves, because
he said 'Budgie, it's you that's got the fuckin' problem with it,
not me.'

I got to Maine Road at 1pm, and when the Newcastle team
bus arrived at 1.30 I went out to greet them. I had a bit of
banter as I ushered them into Maine Road, like I owned the
place, and they were all asking if I was playing and saying they
hoped I got on. I went to the away dressing room and it was
all very strange – sitting having a cup of tea with the lads I had
trained with all week, but who I'd be playing against, even if
it was just to sit on the bench. I went back to the Manchester
City dressing room and got myself ready. I was sitting next to
Tony Coton and I said to him: 'You can come off in any other
game, but don't come off here! I mean it!' He just started
laughing and joking, thinking the same as me – that there was
no chance of it actually happening.

But as I sat watching the game, which was evenly balanced
at 0-0, Tony started shouting over to the bench about 10
minutes before half-time. Tony was a bit of a character and
enjoyed a piss-take, so I assumed he was either pulling my leg
or just wanted water or something. But then he hollered over:
'Budgie – get warmed up, my knee's gone!' No way, I thought,
he's taking the piss. But then at the end of the first half he
collapsed to the ground and was taken off on a stretcher. I
looked at his knee and it was swollen up like a football. It was
a really nasty one.

I was the natural replacement, so it was an unavoidable
situation – I had to play against the team who employed me

and paid my salary. I was also about to become the oldest player ever to play in the Premier League at the tender age of 43 years, 4 months and 26 days. The scale of what was going on hit me at half-time. It was still 0-0 and Brian Horton, the City manager, said: 'C'mon Budgie, keep them out.' That was all I needed to hear. My competitive spirit kicked in.

As I've explained, me and Arthur Cox had a history – he had never forgotten the time I'd climbed out of the window at Derby, and when I came to Newcastle he always reminded me of how much of a traitor I'd been and how I'd let him down. Incidents like that always come back to you in football. I was standing there waiting to be introduced to the crowd at Maine Road – I was nearly 44 years old but I was buzzing so much I felt like I was 24 that day. There was a big crowd of around 30,000, so when the stadium announcer said 'Burridge on for Coton', I ran on, and Arthur Cox was shouting behind me: 'Hey you! Burridge! Cost us the game and we're sacking you!'

Well that fired me up. As I ran on, I shouted back to him: 'Fuck off, I'm winning!' Kevin was standing there next to Arthur, and I could see the anger in his face. He was shifting from foot to foot and I could see he looked very uncomfortable with the situation. He knew questions would be asked if I had a good game and cost Newcastle any points. But I was determined not to let one in – I owed it to Manchester City. I remember running on to the pitch and getting an unbelievable reception from the Newcastle supporters. I'd been a popular player and they knew I'd had a raw deal with Ossie, and they still held me high in their affections. I was getting great support from them and the same from the Manchester City fans, so the whole stadium was cheering for me – with the exception of Arthur, who was still hopping mad on the sidelines, and Kevin, who was cursing the freakish 100-1 shot that had just come in. I didn't know whether to clap the Manchester City fans or clap the Newcastle fans so I just clapped them both.

The game restarted and I remember in the first five minutes Ruel Fox broke away, one-on-one with me. He was very quick, but I had the experience of playing against him every day in training and I knew what he was going to do – he would feint to go left, and take it on the right side. So I went down, worked out what he was going to do and took it clean off his feet. The Man City fans went daft, rising to cheer me. Later in the game, David Ginola cut inside and shaped to shoot, but again I knew what he was going to do – he'd come in from the left side and was going to try and bend it right-footed into my top-left-hand corner, so I anticipated it and caught it. It was a spectacular save and again the City fans went wild. Then Shearer headed one and I kept it out. I made three or four unbelievable saves, and the game finished 0-0. All the Newcastle lads came up to me and said: 'Absolutely brilliant, Budgie.' They were really good sportsmen.

But Newcastle had dropped another two points against a team near the bottom of the table. Thanks to me, their European place was in jeopardy and I was worrying already what was going to be said. After all, one of Newcastle's own coaches had just cost the team two points. I'd been invited up to the press room to speak to journalists, who I knew would be desperate to speak to me as I was headline news on two counts – the oldest man to have played in the Premier League and the man who'd just stiffed his employers!

Kevin Keegan comes across brilliantly to the press with his relaxed manner – apart from that one time when he lost it live on Sky over Alex Ferguson's mind games – but he's one of the worst losers you've ever seen in your life. I only have good things to say about Kevin, but that's just the way he is – he hates losing. I know he hadn't lost that game, but he still had egg on his face for letting me play and I was expecting a rollicking from him. I had gone upstairs to the press room and when I stuck my head round the door Kevin was doing his media conference in front of about 50 press men. I thought 'I don't fancy this, I'm off' and was about to beat a hasty retreat down the stairs, when Kevin spotted me and said: 'Budgie, Budgie, come here.' He sat me down next to him in front of all the journalists and I was shitting myself. But instead of giving me it with both barrels, Kevin started talking me up, saying he knew exactly how I'd perform having watched me every day in training working my backside off. He was saying all these wonderful things about me and using all his charm to handle an awkward situation. But I knew Kevin inside out, I saw him every day in the coaches' room. In front of the press and public he would be very careful with what he said, he was always politically correct, but in the coaches' room he would talk in industrial language and not hold back.

The outcome of it was that when I turned up on the Monday I was still feeling really uneasy and worried about how Kevin would react. When I walked into the training ground, all the Newcastle lads had something to say to me – some saying 'well done', others saying I was a traitor – it was a mixed bag. Ginola was saying to me in his broad French accent: 'Oooo Budgie, fantastique!' while others were not so kind, calling me 'Judas' and saying they should give me a kicking! I didn't know what the coaches were all going to say, so I stuck my head round the door and asked if I could come in. Kevin said: 'Come in and have a cup of tea.' I thought I would be okay, but you could cut the atmosphere with a knife. I don't know if it was my paranoia but it was all very uncomfortable. Kevin was getting a hard time in the local press, with the papers saying he'd been naïve to let me play – an experienced player who knew his opponents inside out. From that day, I was regarded as a bit of a traitor, because it was true – if I hadn't played, Newcastle might have won that game one- or two-nil. It was a horrible feeling, and bad for Newcastle, but it was great for Manchester City. I said to Kevin: 'I'm sorry, but I did warn you that funny things happen in football.' When it started to get splashed all over the local papers it was getting even more embarrassing, and I went to him and asked: 'Do want me to resign, Kevin?' He said: 'No way.'

Kevin was getting it in the neck for playing me, but the newspapers were full of kind words for my performance. In Newcastle, Simon Turnbull's report in the *Northern Echo* after the Manchester City game said:

It boded ill for Newcastle United's European ambitions that the golden oldie who appeared for the second half ended the afternoon as the unchallenged star of the show. When Tony Coton limped off at half-time on Saturday, the odd goalkeeping bird known as Budgie became, at 43, the oldest player to settle on a Premier League perch. That he did so as, simultaneously, City's third-choice goalkeeper and Newcastle's part-time goalkeeping coach made for the kind of human interest story Esther Rantzen might have featured, alongside the feathered, talking Budgies, on *That's Life*.

CHAPTER 21

WONDERWALL

'I couldn't fault Noel and Liam Gallagher; they were really nice. They were just grateful I had helped play a part in saving Manchester City from relegation.'

It was an uncomfortable time for me to be hanging around Newcastle after the 0-0 draw at Maine Road and I was quite happy when I got the chance again for my end-of-the-week escape to Manchester.

The point City had earned against had Newcastle had lifted them out of the bottom four and given the club a renewed sense of belief that they could beat the drop. Our next game was against Aston Villa, another one of my former clubs, and because Tony was in hospital and out for the season I was in line to play again.

Before we got on the coach down to Birmingham for the game, Francis Lee congratulated us on the point we had won against Newcastle on the Saturday. He reminded us that if we won and Leeds beat Crystal Palace on the same night then we would stay up – it would be mission accomplished. He pointed to a huge pile of boxes – every one of them was full of champagne – and he said that they would all be cracked open if we stayed in the Premier League. He gave a really passionate talk and left us in no doubt that this was a massive game for Manchester City and one we had to win. It was putting us under pressure, but he really roused us and we headed down there in a determined frame of mind.

I had played at Villa Park countless times before, but there were none of my old team-mates left from that era – it was a completely different team. The players may have changed, but a lot of the Villa fans remembered me and they gave me a great reception, recognising that I had done well for the club. They were tense as well, because they were in relegation trouble too and just a couple of points above us.

I was buzzing for that game, and was taking my crosses well, kicking it well, handling it well – just feeling great. My confidence soared again when Dean Saunders hit a rasping shot and I tipped it over the bar. But we suffered a major setback when Villa took the lead in a goalmouth scramble. Ugo Ehiogu actually punched the ball into the net with his hand, but the referee hadn't seen it and he gave the goal. City didn't panic, though, and Uwe Rosler equalised just before half-time. Then, with 10 minutes left, Paul Walsh scored for us and we won it 2-1. We'd shown a lot of guts, and when we learned that Palace had been beaten 3-1 at Leeds, it was an absolutely brilliant feeling. We were staying in the Premiership, with two games to spare, and I'd played a part in it – no matter how small. Francis came in with the champagne, as promised, and the celebrations began.

I played the two remaining City games that season. We lost 1-0 to Nottingham Forest at the City Ground, then 3-2 to QPR at Maine Road. As it turned out, it proved to be my last top-flight league game ever. The record stands to this day – the oldest player to have played in the Premier League – because when I faced QPR on 14 May, 1995, I was 43 and 162 days.

There's been a few threatening to take the record over the years, Brad Friedel and David James especially, and I dare say it will tumble one day soon, but I'm proud it has lasted so long.

As I was driving home with Janet after that QPR game I made a snap decision and told her I was not going to play in the Premier League again. I didn't mind playing non-league or lower league football, or heading up to Scotland, but I didn't want to be in that situation again. I felt I'd upset Kevin and betrayed the Newcastle supporters.

I didn't regret a minute of my time at Manchester City though, and the club and the fans have been brilliant to me since that day I came on against Newcastle. About a year later, when I was playing for Queen of the South, I got home from a game in Dumfries and my daughter Katie, who was 14 at the time, came up to me and asked me if I still had any contacts at Manchester City. 'Why, what for?' I asked, like any suspicious parent would. She explained that she wanted tickets for Oasis at Maine Road, and asked me if I could help out because they were like gold dust. I hadn't even heard of Oasis back then. But I did remember a conversation I had had with Francis Lee on the bus back from the Nottingham Forest v City game. He had come over to me and said: 'Look, Budgie, we can't sign you. We owe you for helping us not go down, but we can't offer you a contract. But anything we can help you with in the future, don't hesitate to pick up the phone.'

I thought Katie might be looking for two or three tickets, but she asked for 14! 'Bloody hell,' I thought, but I didn't want to let my daughter down so I rang Francis Lee's secretary, thinking: 'nothing ventured, nothing gained.' Francis was out of the country, but his secretary promised to speak to him about it and get back to me. True to her word, she called me back the next day, but she said she was sorry, but I couldn't have the tickets because it was all sold out. I felt my heart sinking, but then she told me to bring all the girls down to the main entrance at the stadium and ask for Francis.

I hired a minibus and drove all these 14-year-old girls, with Oasis playing on the stereo the whole way from Durham. When I got near the ground, it was about five in the afternoon and I'd never seen so many people. When I drove into the car park, I kept being asked to show my tickets by some stewards, and started to panic a little bit, but when I got to the main entrance I saw one of the City officials that I knew and he told me and the girls to come in.

Francis came down to welcome us then took us to the directors' box and gave the girls some Coca-Colas. It was an amazing sight; the whole of Maine Road was full, including the pitch – there must have been 80,000 people in there. Oasis were due on at 9, and at 7.30 Francis came in and told me and the girls to follow him. We wondered where he was taking us, and it soon became clear – straight to the dressing rooms to meet Noel and Liam Gallagher. I couldn't fault them, they were really nice. They gave the girls T-shirts, signed everything, and it made me cry a little bit seeing my daughter so happy and being treated like royalty. The excitement wasn't over, though. When it got to 9 o'clock, Liam allowed the girls to come with him and sit to the front of the stage. He was so grateful I'd helped play a part in saving City from relegation and he even said during the gig: 'This is the daughter of the boy that helped save us from relegation – John Burridge.' I was in tears; he was singing 'Wonderwall', and it was brilliant.

After the show we were taken to one of the lounges and Ryan Giggs and a few of the Manchester United players had come in. Unbeknown to me, there was a bit of history between Liam Gallagher and Ryan Giggs. A few years before Oasis had become famous, Liam used to work in a car wash. Apparently, Giggsy had driven into the car wash, and when Liam had told him to do one, a big row had broken out between them. So when Giggsy walked in, Liam – who had knocked back a few drinks by this point – started screaming 'Get that arsehole out of here!' I didn't know there was bad blood between them, but I was laughing my head off. I thought it was just because he was a Man Utd player, but the other United players didn't have to leave, just Giggsy. Noel didn't like Giggsy much either, because he'd scored against City on his debut. The whole night was brilliant though and whenever I went back to Manchester City I was always treated like a king. They never forget you there. Maybe I couldn't do the somersaults any more at 43, but I did my best for them. I wish I'd been at City when I was a younger player because it was one of the best clubs I ever played for.

CHAPTER 22

THE BOSS

'It is exactly the same drain on your time and energy managing Blyth Spartans as it is managing Real Madrid – the only difference is the number of noughts at the end of cheques.'

I knew from the age of 15 when I first went into football as a professional that one day I would be a manager or a coach. I also knew I'd be in football until the day I died. I really hope I die on the football field or the training ground – although not just yet! I'm really in love with the game. Football makes me what I am; I'm not a person who's introvert and keeps myself to myself, football makes me happy. I like to see people play football with a smile on their face. I hate to see these people who go on to a football field all serious and nervous. I knew I could take that enjoyment into coaching and I'd always known I wanted to be in football until the day they put me in a box.

After my last game for Man City I was inundated with calls from so many teams – Third Division, Fourth Division, Scottish league, all wanting me to play on – it was incredible. I turned most of them down, but when I was approached by Blyth Spartans it was hard to resist – they were only about 20 minutes' drive away from my house. They played in the Northern Premier

League and were managed by Peter Harrison. We came to an arrangement where I was allowed to stay on and continue working at Newcastle, and by that time I had also started dividing my coaching time by taking the goalkeepers at Leeds United for a couple of days a week.

I didn't want to go back into league football, so the arrangement was perfect. I couldn't deny that I still wanted to play, because even though I was 47 I was as fit as a fiddle. I played a year with Blyth before they sacked Peter Harrison in March 1997. I was viewed as a big name locally, and it was well known that I had my coaching badges, so I was approached by their chairman who asked if I'd be interested in taking over from Peter. I pointed out to him that I had coaching commitments at Newcastle and Leeds, but he was happy to accommodate them. At the back of my mind I already knew my workload was heavy enough, but I couldn't resist the idea and said I would have a go at it. I'd had 30-odd years of being on the receiving end of managers' words, so I thought I'd try the boot on the other foot. But when you are a part-time manager it is far more difficult than being a full-time boss. My workload was already unbelievable at Newcastle, and that was made worse by the fact that I was driving down to Leeds twice a week to train the future England keepers Nigel Martyn and Paul Robinson, and then playing for Blyth on a Saturday.

In management, the job never ever stops – Arthur Cox and Kevin Keegan had always told me that was the case. It is exactly the same drain on your time and energy managing Blyth Spartans as it is managing Real Madrid – the only difference is the number of noughts at the end of cheques. Kevin and Arthur warned me that I would be taking on an awful lot by getting into management and I soon realised they were right. The phone never stops, even at non-league level. You're constantly thinking about what you are going to do for training. I used to finish training at Leeds, drive all the way back up to Newcastle, then head straight to Blyth.

I used to make sure my players were paid £150 a week – a big salary at the time in that league for part-time players, because all the other clubs were only paying their boys £50 a week. But it wasn't just a case of turning up and collecting a pay packet – they had to work hard for it, and harder than anyone else in the league. I insisted that they had to train Monday, Tuesday and Thursday to earn their money. Under previous regimes they had expected to just come in on a Tuesday and Thursday, have a quick eight-a-side game and then go home. But it wasn't like that with Budgie, being the stickler that I am. We used to play on a Saturday, then we would all be back in on a Monday in the gym at Gateshead Sports Centre. I'd make them do upper-body work and fitness routines. I'd do all the gym training with them, then we would head outside for a bit of cross-country to build up stamina, after that we'd go onto the track and do some short, sharp sprinting. They'd be knackered and moaned their heads off about it, but I'd quickly remind them that they could go and play for someone else for £50 a week. I was also quick to point out that it was making them all better players. I was only being professional in my approach and we were the fittest team in the league by far. I'd had my gripes about Ron Saunders and Alex Miller, but both were sticklers for players working hard at training and they taught me well in that respect.

On the Tuesday training nights we would work on tactics – defensive duties then a game of five-a-side. On Thursday nights the emphasis would be on attacking, then another five-a-side. It was a full-time job really, but I made it that way for myself. The self-imposed workload was too much and it wore me out. I did two years of that and it started to take its toll. I was knackered at the end of each week. I was getting older, even if I wouldn't admit it to myself.

Football management is a business and, like any other business, you are called into boardrooms and expected to give your input. People would say: 'Budgie, we're £30,000 in debt, we've got VAT bills to pay – what are we going to do about it?' Some people are oblivious to all that side of football – they think it's just a case of turning up on a Saturday and playing, but when you become a manager everything is heaped upon your shoulders. To sort out our financial problems, I arranged for Newcastle to bring their full team to Croft Park for a pre-season fund-raiser. Shearer, Ginola, Fox, Lee, Bracewell, Albert – they all came and helped to pack the place out. We had 8,000 people in Croft Park and we raked in about £25,000 in gate receipts. With one gate, I'd paid off the VAT bill. I also asked Howard Wilkinson to bring Leeds United for another friendly, and they brought a team that included Viduka, Kewell, Hasselbaink, Martyn, and all their stars. We pulled in another full house and another thirty grand, so I'd paid the wage bill and put money in the bank for the club. I was told in the boardroom: 'Budgie, you're a miracle worker, well done.' But I responded with: 'Yeah, thanks, but don't forget I might want a player out of that money.'

You were never able to switch off from the job. Every spare night I had I'd be watching a game, at Spennymoor or Bishop Auckland, or watching future opponents and trying to get a tactical edge over them. I would even go to watch pub teams on a Sunday just to see if there were quality players who had slipped the net and not come to anyone's attention. I would constantly be on the phone to Middlesbrough or Sunderland pestering them to see if they had any youngsters on the radar, or a club like Darlington and Hartlepool trying to get players to Blyth on loan. Bryan Robson would call me and tell me there was a player at Boro I should watch, and I would say: 'Put him in the reserves and I'll come and have a look at him tonight.' Before I knew it I'd be in the car driving to Manchester to watch a reserves game for a player who may or not be an asset to my team, getting back late at night. It was an unbelievable workload, but you become blinded to how much you are doing. You become obsessed with wanting to make the team better. It was even worse for me because I was player-manager. I found it much harder to go out and concentrate on my game when I had the rest of the team to worry about, as well as tactics and substitutions as the game unfolded.

After two years, I went to the Blyth chairman and said: 'I can't do this any more. I can't continue like this – I'm dying, it's killing me. I'm working my backside off at Newcastle and Leeds with my goalkeeping jobs. I really enjoy the management side of things but it's taking my life away.'

I was obviously getting more money for coaching at Newcastle and Leeds but it felt like I was doing 20 times the work at Blyth. It was a part-time job in name, but being a manager is a full-time job, it's 24 hours. I've seen strong characters like Kevin Keegan ground down by football management. I saw him come into Newcastle a relatively young man, joining in training every day and with a smile on his face, and then I saw him walk out of there years later with grey hair, looking like he was carrying the weight of the world on his shoulders.

It was gruelling work, but I had a fantastic time at Blyth. I took them through all the qualifying rounds for the FA Cup, and as we were listening to the draw on the team bus coming back from our final qualifying game, fate played its hand and drew my old club Blackpool out of the hat. I was a household name in Blackpool and in their Hall of Fame, so it was as big as it could get for me – my old club at Bloomfield Road.

Because of my connection with Blackpool, the newspapers were really talking up the game. Tickets were selling like hot cakes and in the build-up to the match we even had a royal visit to the ground – The Duke of York, Prince Andrew. The *Journal* newspaper reported: 'Self-confessed royalist "Budgie" Burridge said: "The Duke's knowledge of the game is fantastic, and he was very interested in the finances of the club. He wished us all the best for Saturday and his visit has certainly helped our confidence."'

On the day of the match, the media hype cranked up another notch. The tie was generating unbelievable interest. Part of the broadcasting deal we had signed to generate some extra cash for the club gave the TV cameras access to our dressing room and let them film all of our behind-the-scenes preparations. That created a lot of extra exposure for us and took us way out of our regular routine. I was a firm believer in the Magic of the Cup, but as a manager I found it all a bit irritating. I didn't like that a lot of the focus was on me. I wanted it to be all about Blyth Spartans' day out, not me. I know it was unavoidable because I was a former Blackpool player, but this was one day that I could have done without being in the spotlight so much.

I had to get up much earlier than usual to do all the press and TV interviews, and by the time I went out to play I was totally and utterly drained, mentally and physically. I could really have done without all the added hassle, but I had to do right by the club because every penny counted. It was helluva cup tie, and we didn't let anyone down with the performance we gave. You can still see the game on YouTube now – it's a humdinger. We were 1-0 down within four minutes, and I can be seen having a little difference of opinion with my defenders, but the lads were magnificent and we went in 2-1 ahead at half-time and with a huge upset on the cards. I kept the boys calm during the interval, cracked a few jokes and told them just to continue with the gameplan and not let Blackpool frighten them, no matter how much pressure they applied. As expected, Blackpool threw everything at us in the second half and clawed their way into a 3-2 lead, before we got a late equaliser. It looked like we'd snatched a replay, and with it a good few thousand pounds more for the club. But there was a sting in the tail for us, and they scored again in the last minute. It was a classic FA Cup tie and even though we lost I was so proud of the lads and told every one of them that in the dressing room.

That was the undoubted pinnacle of my time as a manager, but the day-to-day stuff was hard going and you soon find that you can't be everyone's pal when you're the boss. Part-time players are notorious for going out for a couple of bevvies on a Friday night and I had to stop all that and threaten to sack people if they broke the code of discipline.

We had a lad called Keith Fletcher, a brilliant player who had international caps with Grenada in the Caribbean, but he was a laid-back character and a bugger for going out clubbing on a Friday night. I was paying him £150 a week and was hearing all these stories about him being out on the razz before games. I got sick of it and decided I couldn't just turn a blind eye to it. I asked the board if I could start putting them in a hotel the night before a game where I could keep an eye on them, but the club didn't have that kind of money to splash around, so I had to think of other ways to put a stop to the drinking culture. I used to have these little breathalyser bags on the coach and on Saturday mornings, if I thought somebody was looking a bit groggy, I'd pull them into the corner and tell them to blow into the bag. If they'd had anything to drink on the Friday night it would show up straight away. I would fine them £50 on the spot and if I thought it was bad enough I wouldn't play them.

It's a notorious problem among part-time players because they've been working hard in their day jobs all week. I suppose that's why a lot of them are part-time players and not professionals. Certainly, a lot of them had the ability to go further in the game, but not the hunger to push themselves on. I used to get complaints all the time from the chairman about me being too harsh on the players. But the way I saw it, they were getting paid three times more than any other team in the league and I wasn't asking them too much, just to stay in one night of the week and rest up for the game; then post-match on a Saturday they could do whatever they wanted.

Football was already heading into a new era of professionalism in the 1990s and in the top leagues the habit of playing together and drinking together was coming to an end. When I was playing you always used to get a few bevvies on the coach, especially if we'd won away from home. But I was used to travelling on professional coaches, and getting stuck into the drink was no longer the done thing. When I first arrived at Blyth we would stop at the first off-licence we saw, everybody would stick a tenner in and they'd have half-a-dozen beers on the way home, but times had changed. I viewed things exactly the same way as the professionals and I cut out the drinking. The chairman would be trying to fork out £100 to buy five or six cases of beer, but being the professional I was, I stopped it. I would have blazing arguments with the

chairman, who would always side with the players. He'd say:
'C'mon, Budgie – they've worked all week, they've stayed in
on a Friday like you've asked them. Let them have a drink will
you?' But I would stick to my guns, and say that once they
were out of my sight they could do whatever they liked.

It was a sure-fire way to create bad feeling, I can see that
now. The lads were pissed off with me and I got myself a bit
disliked. Looking back on it, I realise that I should have cut
them a bit of slack and I was too harsh. They weren't
professionals earning thousands of pounds a week, they were
guys earning £150 a week on top of their weekly wage for
their day job, and I took the discipline a bit too far by not
allowing them to have a drink on the way home. I should have
realised that, but at the time I wanted them to think like me.
My strictness was more suited to a professional club than
Blyth Spartans. My discipline and training regime was tough
on them, no doubt about it. If I'd been at a professional club
I'd have been even harsher though – I'd have had players
training twice a day, especially with the money they were on. I
was prepared to put that level of dedication in myself so I
suppose I expected it back from others who I worked with.
With my outlook I probably shouldn't have operated at part-
time level, because I asked too much of them, which wasn't
fair. But you have to start somewhere.

I enjoyed being a manager, though, and I was a good
organiser and good tactically. But the days of a player-manager
are well and truly gone now. It was too tough for me then, and
you don't see many managers nowadays trying to juggle the
two roles. When I was in the middle of a game I'd be trying to
concentrate on my own game, but if there was an injury or we
needed a tactical reshuffle, my mind had to switch to becoming
a manager again and I had to think quickly. It was difficult.

But I loved the experience of managing and there were some good people at Blyth. The fans we took to Blackpool were tremendous. The passion you find in non-league clubs is just the same as you would find at a Premier League club – especially in the boardroom. If there are backers who have put hundreds of pounds into clubs then they want a say – just the same as bigger fish in the professional leagues. Like I say, it's only the noughts at the end of the cheques that separates them. But in my case, I was constantly arguing with the board about money or arguing with them about the way I was treating the boys, so I thought 'I've had enough of this'. It eventually got under my skin when I heard people complaining about hard training, especially when I was working so hard myself, so I just had to get out of it.

CHAPTER 23

STRESSED AND DEPRESSED

*'I had another major helping of grief to deal with
when right out of the blue I was arrested.'*

As the strain of managing Blyth started to get on top of me I
was becoming narky and I wasn't myself at all. My job at
Newcastle was bugging me too. I would see people getting paid
twice as much money as me and doing five times less. I won't
name names...no, sod it, this is my book, so I *will* name names!
In my opinion, Kevin Keegan's assistant Terry McDermott did
bugger all. I didn't really see what Arthur Cox and the reserve
coach Jeff Clarke did a lot of the time either. I respected Arthur
a lot for his dedication to football, even though our fall-out saw
me crossed off his Christmas card list, but I sometimes thought
they were just there because they were Kevin's friends. You
would see them sitting have a cup of tea in the coaches' room or
picking up cones on the training ground while I was busy
working my bollocks off. The first team coach, Derek
Fazackerley, used to take all the serious training, while Kevin did
all the organising, so I never knew what Terry actually did. I'd go
out on to the training ground in the pissing rain, and I would see

Terry and a couple of the others just sitting round drinking tea. They would then go out, have a laugh and pick up a few cones and balls, then go back inside and have their dinner after training. They were getting big salaries and I felt they were hangers-on.

Football clubs always have people like Terry McDermott and Jeff Clarke and I came across plenty of them during my career. Sometimes it would make me mad, because I felt that certain coaches maybe didn't have the same knowledge and dedication as me, but had sneaked into top jobs largely because of their friends and connections. I think in my case people could be a bit frightened of my personality and that's why I was no stranger to friction and arguments. I would always fight my corner, and sometimes it would cost me my job. But I would rather stand up for my principles than become an arse-kisser. There were Yes Men at Newcastle who would just say: 'Yes Kevin, that's right Kevin, anything you say Kevin.' To me, that was neglecting an important job within the football club, because on the odd occasion Kevin's judgment was maybe a bit out he could have benefited from a strong second opinion.

There was at least one occasion when I got a serious telling-off from Kevin and nearly got the sack over it. Our first-choice keeper, Pavel Srnicek, was not the bravest goalie in the world – he was a fantastic shot-stopper and you couldn't get the ball past him in training, but when he had to come for crosses he had a tendency to shut his eyes and hope for the best. I'm not for a second here knocking Pav's ability, he was a cracking keeper for Newcastle, but in my eyes there was no excuse for him not being fully committed when he was involved in 50-50 challenges. I told him he shouldn't hold back – if he got his teeth knocked out, it wouldn't be the end of the world. At least he would have stopped a goal and earned the respect of his team-mates. I was telling him to take one for the team and I would keep on at him in training. Kevin would say: 'Budgie, calm down' and I'd protest – 'But Kev, he's behaving like a coward.' It definitely led to a bit of unease between us.

It came to a head when were away in Eastern Europe for a Uefa Cup tie. It was a horrible wet and windy night. Someone sent a cross in and I could see that Pavel was in two minds about whether to come for it. The ball held up in the wind and, as Pav stayed rooted to his line, I saw the centre-forward was hell-bent on getting on the end of it. Pav hesitated and the forward got to it first and headed it in. Newcastle got a 1-1 draw, which wasn't a bad result, but when we were in the dressing room afterwards I just couldn't bite my lip and turn a blind eye to the goal we had lost. Kevin was going round telling the lads 'well done' and then he asked if anyone had anything to say. I couldn't help myself and chirped up: 'Fucking hell, Pav, you should have punched the forward's head off there.' Kevin wasn't happy with me and Pav got upset and went to see him about it later. Kevin hauled me into his office and said: 'Budgie, you shouldn't have said that in public.' But I wasn't in the mood for backing down and I pleaded: 'But Kev, I was only telling the truth – he should have gone right through him.' Kevin basically gave me a yellow card, and told me the next time I opened my mouth in the dressing room and said something against Pavel I'd be sacked. I just had to take my medicine – he was the boss – but I thought to myself that the days of being able to say it is as it is, as long as it's constructive, were over. I prefer a bit of honesty. That's when I knew political correctness was starting to creep into football, which I hate.

My life was starting to unravel a bit, and it took a turn for the worse when I had my post at Leeds taken away from me too.

The job at Leeds had come about after they bought Nigel Martyn from Crystal Palace – the first keeper in English football to be sold for £1 million. I'd known Nigel since he was a kid, so Howard Wilkinson called me up and asked if I could come down to Leeds and do a couple of days each week training with him and their young keeper Paul Robinson. I had to ask Kevin first, but he was great about it and said it would be no problem. We always had Monday off at Newcastle anyway and Wednesday was usually my day with the reserves, so I could just hook up with them later after spending a morning or afternoon down at Leeds' training ground. The arrangement worked very well at first, and I was able to juggle my Leeds commitments with my main job at Newcastle. But when Howard Wilkinson was sacked towards the end of 1996, I was left high and dry when they brought in George Graham.

He had done absolutely brilliant at Arsenal, but he'd been out of football since he was sacked and banned for accepting a back-hander from an agent. He was back in the big time at Leeds, but there was bad blood between us from our time together at Crystal Palace, when I had booted him at half-time because I felt he wasn't trying hard enough. That incident was just one of those dressing room arguments that boiled over – they're usually forgotten about within a day or two, but I never really did make my peace with George after it happened. George was coming to the end of his career when he played for Palace, and I had gone for him in this particular game because I felt he was just strutting around and spraying passes when it took his fancy, rather than getting stuck in. We'd been losing at half-time, and I had laid the blame on him for posing around. He took exception to it, and the next thing we're rolling around on the dressing room floor trying to knock hell out of each other. He'd been used to being the big cheese at Arsenal and Manchester United and when he came to Palace, which was largely full of kids, I think he probably thought he could pretty much do as he pleased without anyone questioning him. He hadn't banked on me though, and if I thought someone wasn't pulling their weight – as I did that day – then I wasn't going to just sit there and say nothing, especially if I'd been sweating blood myself.

So I knew what was coming as soon as he walked through the door at Elland Road, because I was well aware that he didn't like me. He has a very strong personality, like me, and when we were in the same company we collided. You can't have two personalities like that at the same club. But he was the manager and I was only the part-time goalkeeping coach, so there was only going to be one winner at Leeds United and it wasn't going to be me. If it had been a fight I would have battered him, but this was different, this was politics within a football club, and he used his power and didn't waste much time in sacking me.

What really annoyed me was that he got Nigel Martyn to do his dirty work. He told poor Nigel: 'Either you tell Budgie that he's finished here or I will.' Nigel thought it would be a hundred times more tactful coming from him, as I regarded him as a friend, and was probably well aware that I would have smacked George on the chin, so he came up to me and said: 'Sorry, Budgie, this is the end. George says he doesn't want you here. I want you here, but it's not my call.' Nigel was a nice lad, so I slapped him on the back and told him not to worry about it. I wished him well in his career and promised to stay in touch, which I have done to this day. He had a good career too, and would have won more than his 23 caps for England if he'd stayed injury free. It was a pleasure to work with him.

My Leeds job was gone, then the Newcastle job went, and then I had another major helping of grief to deal with when right out of the blue I was arrested.

It all came about through my involvement with a couple of sports shops I ran with Janet in the North East. I had opened them as a business sideline, and as well as running the shops, Janet and I would set up market stalls and sell the stuff. We would sell all the usual branded sportswear and football shirts, plus a bit of designer gear too. Most of it was bankrupt stock or rejects that had slight imperfections, and we would flog them on at knock-down prices. We used to buy in lots from a warehouse in Manchester, and I would take carloads down to Leeds and sell a few things down there. We did okay out of it, and it gave us a nice boost to our income, but then one day it all came to an abrupt end. I got the dreaded knock at the door and the police came to the house and arrested me, accusing me of selling fake goods. It was a horrible experience, and it knocked me for six.

It turned out they had been acting on some kind of anonymous tip-off, and the trading standards officers had been tailing me and putting me under surveillance for weeks. They even had video footage of all the lads at Blyth kitted out in my gear when we went to play Blackpool in the FA Cup, so the tabloids were lapping it all up!

It was an honest mistake, though. We'd bought £20,000 worth of what we thought was legitimate reject stock, but the goods actually turned out to be fakes. The trading standards folk wanted to throw the book at me and they took me to the Magistrates Court. I was really bitter about it at the time because I knew for a fact that a big supermarket chain had bought 10 times the amount I had from the same supplier, but all they got was a slap on the wrist. It was only 20 grand's worth of stuff, which may sound a lot of money but it wasn't in terms of the business. The supermarket had bought a whole warehouse-worth and pretty much got off scot-free, while I was being treated like a criminal.

Being John Burridge, the court case was a big story at the time for the press. They were making out I was a bit of a Flash Harry, and even reported that I'd driven off after the hearing in my jeep with personalised plates. Yes, I had a personalised registration number – my number plate was A 5AVE – but, so what? It didn't make me criminal kingpin, did it?

I was fined nearly £16,000 and I left the court feeling sick and depressed.

CHAPTER 24

THE PRIORY TO THE LIFE OF REILLY

*'Not to put too fine a point on it, I became mentally
ill. I knew I had to get away from England.'*

It was a feeling I thought I would never experience, but for the
first time in my life I felt like I needed to get out of football,
and get out of England, or I would end up losing my mind.

I felt suffocated after my energy-sapping spell in management
at Blyth. I did enjoy the job immensely, up to a point, but it got
to the intolerable stage where I ended up feeling like I was
working myself towards an early grave. It was my own fault for
trying to do too much and I'm not blaming anyone else. I tried
to juggle the demands of being a manager with my coaching jobs
at Leeds and Newcastle and helping out with the sportswear
shops too. My state of mind was already fragile enough, but the
court case over selling counterfeit goods was probably the straw
that broke the camel's back. Even though I felt that I was being
made a scapegoat, I was ashamed to see my name plastered over
all the headlines. I became paranoid that people were staring at
me and talking about me in the street. People who should have
known better seemed happy to judge me without having all the

facts, and I knew they all just thought I was on the fiddle. I would probably have felt the same in their shoes, but it's really hard to take when you're on the receiving end.

Not to put too fine a point on it, I became mentally ill. I was overworked and way too stressed and eventually that made me suicidal. My age had finally caught up with me and my football career, and I knew there would be no turning the clock back and walking into a top team as their keeper again, even if I had wanted to. I had worked myself into the ground and gone a bit doolally. Weeks after I finished with Blyth, I just wanted to die. As I outlined at the start of the book, I sat in my room for three or four days at a time and wouldn't come out. I really didn't care if I died.

After I'd been overpowered in my bedroom, injected in the bum with a sedative and dumped in the Priory, my first thought when I came to was to hatch an escape plan. The staff you find in these places are well trained in how to deal with difficult patients, and I'm sure I would have come firmly into that category in those first few weeks. I must have been a pain in the arse. The fact that I'd been sectioned meant that I couldn't just stroll through the front door and go home. I was there for a reason – to make me better – and it took me a bit of time to adjust and get my head around that. It wasn't exactly *One Flew Over the Cuckoo's Nest* though, and if you showed the right attitude, then the staff did everything they could to help you get yourself together and get well again.

They started giving me some medication and I calmed down and became an easier patient to deal with. I had the odd setback, but after my initial freak-out at finding myself in there, I started to get a bit better each day. After a while, trust grew on both sides, and I would be allowed to put on my training kit and do a bit of training to help with my therapy.

There was one day when I accidentally went out of the gates at the Priory and set off a full-scale alarm. I had only been planning to go for a 20-minute run – 10 minutes there and 10 minutes back – but as I was jogging down the road, I looked round and could see doctors coming after me and a nurse screaming at the top of her voice: 'Johhhhhhn, come back!' They thought I was trying to make a break for it. The nurse had been about 400 yards behind me when I first spotted her, but after I'd jogged on a bit, the next thing I knew she was grabbing hold of my arm – she must have been some sort of Olympic athlete to catch me because I was quite a fast runner! They took me back and even though I tried to explain to them that I only wanted to go for a run and I was planning to come back, they put a black mark against me and had me down as a potential escapee. I think I got double medication after that for a few days to stop me in my tracks.

After my group therapy, where I heard the poor woman's tragic tale about losing her husband and her children in a car crash, I dug deep and got my head properly together. I had positive ideas swimming about my mind, and I just needed to harness them. The healthiest outlook I felt I could take was to try and somehow get a fresh start. I became determined to look forward and not back. I knew I definitely had to get away from England, or I'd run the risk of lapsing right back into depression.

When I came out of the Priory after three months, I thought that there had to be a better life than working your bollocks off, and not for a fortune either. I was lying on the settee one day and thought to myself: 'There's more to life than this. I'm sick of it pissing down and blowing a gale.' And that's when I started thinking about opportunities abroad.

Because I had my coaching licence, I took the bull by the horns and rang up the Scottish Football Association – where I had sat all my badges – and told them I was keen on a move abroad. They were really helpful and printed off a form and sent it to me in Durham, which I filled out and returned. After giving it a bit of thought, my first choice was America, my second choice was Australia and my third choice was Dubai. The SFA uploaded my CV and preferred destinations on to the FIFA coaching page, along with all my details, background and qualifications, and I didn't have to wait long before I got a call. I was delighted to hear the voice of my old boss at Sheffield United, Ian Porterfield.

Ian said he'd noticed from the website that I might want to come to Dubai. 'I can't help you there, Budgie,' he told me, 'but I can do the next best thing – I'm just a few hours away in Oman.' I was upfront with him and explained to him that I'd been in hospital, but he said that wasn't a problem and he asked me to come out and see him. I had nothing to lose, so I thought 'what the hell', and a few days later Janet and I got on a plane to Muscat. We stayed in a lovely hotel, and were immediately taken by how friendly the people were. The setting was stunning – sunshine, mountains and beaches, and I was well impressed with all the heritage the place had to offer. I thought it was paradise. I had a good chat with Ian, who was in charge of the national team, and he told me he wanted me to come and join his backroom staff as goalkeeping coach. There wasn't much to think about – it was an offer I couldn't possibly refuse. We kept the house on in Durham in case we ever returned, but our bags were packed for a new life.

To begin with, the team wasn't that good and the federation wasn't the most organised, but the lifestyle was absolutely wonderful and it was just what I needed at that time. I had gone from the Priory to living the life of Reilly. Unfortunately, the national team's results were poor and Ian Porterfield was sacked. Coaches weren't given long to get results, and unless they somehow put together an immediate winning run, then they would be dispensed with. I was panicking – I thought I would be out too because it had been Ian who had brought me in, but the Oman FA were honourable people and not only were they happy to keep me on, but they let me take the national team for a few games while they looked for Ian's successor. I was happy enough just doing the job on a caretaker basis, because I thought if I took the job permanently it would be like signing my death warrant. It was the kind of job that had a very short lifespan. After Ian's departure, they first appointed a Brazilian coach, Valdeir Vieira, who was only in the post for a year between 1998 and 1999. He had been a career coach rather than a famous player, but when he left they got one of the biggest names in world football – the brilliant full-back from Brazil's 1970 World Cup-winning team, Carlos Alberto Torres. We got on like a house on fire, and I really enjoyed working under him. He didn't speak an awful lot of English, but we were able to communicate and he had a brilliant sense of humour.

I found the work really rewarding and I did my best to embrace the culture of Oman, even learning Arabic and a bit of Swahili! Some of the favourite sayings that I would use to coach my goalkeepers were 'Ruah alla Toule' (go straight), 'Fawk alla Toule' (get up), 'Ascut' (be quiet), 'Box Filwadga' (punch him in the face) and 'Murafani a Hafa Alrwajoul ila mustashfa' (rough translation: 'next time, put this man in hospital!').

Even learning a few simple words of the local lingo shows that you are willing to make an effort, and my coaching style was always to talk to the players and encourage them the best I could. It earned me their respect. I couldn't have stood the thought of having to go through a translator all the time; it would have frustrated the hell out of me and it's not my style anyway. I prefer to communicate with people directly.

I had been coaching in Oman for a couple of years, and was even still playing for the Army team to keep my fitness up, when my life was once again turned upside down. I had a near-death experience, and I consider myself very lucky to have survived.

I was on the road cycling back from a weight training session in the gym one day, when a van pulled in front of me in the cycle lane. Its door swung open without any warning and as I swerved to avoid it I was hit by a car travelling at 70mph in the opposite direction. I don't remember much, but I was knocked off my bike and dragged for 50 yards underneath the car.

My body was battered beyond recognition. The damage I suffered was pretty gruesome and all the medical work I needed does not make for pleasant reading: I had a partially severed left ear, 147 stitches in my face, umpteen operations and skin grafts, 14 damaged teeth, a severely damaged shoulder, a damaged nervous system and one arm was left shorter than the other. People started calling me Steve Austin after the Six Million Dollar Man. But I was the Six Million Dollar Man and the Bionic Budgie all mashed into one!

After that, I was registered 35 per cent disabled and became hooked on Prozac to keep my nerves together. I also needed a hell of a lot of counselling. I had spent my whole life priding myself on my fitness, so it was a bitter pill to swallow. I felt like an invalid, and having found such a good life in Oman I felt I was back to square one. It was a terrible time, and I owe a lot to all those who got me through it. Thankfully, there was no question of me having to go home to England. My job was safe and everyone rallied round to make sure I got back on my feet.

I'll never be allowed to say who was responsible for the

accident, as I took them to court – backed by the PFA – and won compensation, but it was somebody high-profile. I'm just glad that justice was done and that my body was strong enough to heal to some extent. Lifting all those hay bales when I was 12, and a lifetime of weight training, had prepared me for the worst, and thankfully I lived to tell the tale.

CHAPTER 25

A STAR IS BORN

*'The thing that struck me most about Ali Al-Habsi
was that his dedication matched mine.'*

I got a lot of satisfaction from coaching goalkeepers in Oman – they were eager to learn, and to watch them take on board what you've taught them and see them make progress before your eyes makes you very proud. It wasn't long before I discovered my star pupil. I saw this 14-year-old lad playing in goal for a Third Division side and straight away I thought he was fantastic. He couldn't speak a word of English and was huge for his age. His name was Ali Al-Habsi, and he would go on to become the first player from the Gulf to make it in the English Premier League, first with Bolton and then on loan at Wigan.

I took him under my wing and when I brought him to train with the first team, everyone thought I was crazy. The thing that struck me most about Ali Al-Habsi was that his dedication matched mine. When he was still at school, he lived 15 miles outside Muscat, but he would catch a ramshackle minibus to come and train with me. At 5am he would run one kilometre to the training ground, where I would have the cones set up, ready to put him through his paces before the sun got too hot. He did that every day for a year and a half and I knew he was going to be a professional.

I obviously still had a lot of contacts in England, so I rang Sir Alex Ferguson up at Manchester United, told him I thought the kid could make the grade, and arranged to bring him over for a trial. I went to the federation and asked for them to subsidise two plane tickets, and when they said no, I paid for them myself. We went over to the UK and I took him to United's training centre at Carrington for a fortnight's trial, where he was mixing in the company of stars like Ole Gunnar Solskjaer and Ruud van Nistelrooy. I was standing behind the goal, talking to him in Arabic, and when he stood up to a hefty challenge from Van Nistelrooy I shouted to him: 'Good, young man!'

Sir Alex thought he was brilliant, but because he was so young there was no way United could arrange a work permit for him, and reluctantly they had to drop their interest. The same problem arose when Manchester City were keen, but I kept trying and took him to Bolton where Sam Allardyce was the manager at the time. Sam is a very intelligent fella, and he worked out that if Ali played in another country for a couple of years, he would be able to build up his number of appearances with the national team and satisfy the demands of obtaining a work permit in the UK. So Ali Al-Habsi went to Lynn Oslo for a couple of years, and proved a sensation there, while also playing the 75 per cent of national games that you needed at the time to come to Britain on a work permit.

However, during my time trying to find Ali a club, I was sacked by the Oman FA – basically for sticking up for him in a row with the national coach. Carlos Alberto had left by this time and they had a Czech coach called Milan Macala, with whom I never really saw eye-to-eye. By this time, Ali Al-Habsi had left school and got a job as a fireman, while we tried to get him a professional football club. But when I brought him back to Oman, Macala called him to one side and, in full earshot of me, said: 'Ali, don't pay heed to what John is saying to you. You will never be a professional player, you will be back here crying because you don't have a job. In my country, the Czech Republic, we have 20 goalkeepers better than you.'

When I overheard what Macala was telling him, I went berserk and punched him in the face. He was not only undermining me, he was doing Ali a massive disservice. I was hauled before the federation the next day, after Macala complained that I had physically assaulted him. I fought my corner and said he shouldn't be saying things like that to a 16-year-old kid, even if he did feel he wasn't any good. They said they didn't want me to take Ali out of the federation and away to another country, but I said they couldn't stop me. I didn't like what I was hearing and told them: 'Sack me then, I don't care.'

I was without a job again, but not for long – I was soon approached by the biggest club in the region, Al Ain, and they gave me a great job in Abu Dhabi. The only problem was that it was too far away to commute on a daily basis, and I more or less had to live away from my wife for three years.

While I settled into my job, Ali Al-Habsi went from strength to strength. He was voted the best goalkeeper in Norway two years running and my phone never stopped – I had Souness from Newcastle, Houllier from Liverpool, Stuart Pearce from City and Sir Alex from United all wanting to sign him, but I had shaken hands on a deal with Sam Allardyce. They were all offering crazy money because Ali was hot property, but I had to honour my handshake to Sam. Ali's done brilliantly since he went to England and he hasn't even reached his peak as a goalkeeper.

Abu Dhabi is still enormously rich and the Al Ain Football Club is the focus of a lot of the wealth in the region. Because Al Ain is the same distance inland from Dubai and Oman, it was a popular place. The chairman of the football club is the older brother of the Manchester City owner Sheikh Mansour – Sheikh Hazza bin Zayed Al Nahyan, so you could imagine the kind of money we are talking about. Al Ain, in reality, are probably as rich as Manchester United. They only get 8,000 people at their games, but they have Sheik Hazza's money bankrolling them and he probably has enough to buy United, and have plenty of change left over.

The job at Al Ain was fantastic and I was on mega money, but I found it a hard place to live because I prefer to be next to the sea. After being so settled in Oman, I found in comparison there was not a lot going on in Al Ain – it really was the middle of the desert. When you're inland in the desert, there is not much to do outdoors to keep your mind occupied because it can become unbearably hot. I was put up in fantastic accommodation, but I missed Janet, who couldn't join me because she was busy pursuing her own career as an estate agent back in Muscat. Al Ain was only about a three-hour drive from Oman, but that's way too far to be commuting back and forward each day, and I just had to stay there when I was working and pop back to Muscat whenever I could.

The culture in Abu Dhabi was an eye-opener, and I learned something new every day. The Sheikhs would do all their business between Saturday and Wednesday, then return to Al Ain on a Thursday and Friday, which is the weekend in the Middle East. Saturday is like a Monday morning in Britain, and that's how it works. The Sheikhs might drive to Al Ain to spend time with one of their four wives, but having so many wives would be an expensive life. If you buy one wife a Rolex or a Rolls-Royce then you have to buy the other three exactly the same. That's the rules, and you have to be a very wealthy man to have four wives. People will read this and think that's horrible, but that's just their culture – it's different and who are we to say it's wrong? It's very much a man's world here though. There are no laws like England, where the wife gets half of the wealth in a divorce. Here, you only have to tell her in public three times, on three separate occasions, in front of friends and witnesses, that you want a divorce. I wasn't shocked by any of this; I just find other cultures fascinating. I've lived here so long now, I know all the rules and regulations inside out and I'm used to it.

Working with the players could be a weird and wonderful experience too. One day a player, who was meant to be a full-time professional, came up to me and told me bold as brass: 'I won't be in at training tomorrow; I'm taking my mum shopping in Dubai.' I couldn't believe what I was hearing and told him he needed to come in to do some weight training. He obviously feared his mother more than he feared me because he said he still wasn't coming. When I fined him a week's wages for missing training, he was straight on the phone to the Sheikh to complain. Imagine something like that happening under Ron Saunders or Alex Miller! I must say though, the attitude of players in the Gulf has come on in leaps and bounds since then and they have started to grasp what being a professional means and the rewards that hard work and dedication can bring.

I loved my job in Al Ain, but I couldn't bear being apart from Janet and I missed Muscat. The Oman FA re-hired me, and I returned to work under their new German coach Bernd Stange. It was my association with Stange – a brilliant character – that led to the most bizarre job offer I had ever received...to go and work for Saddam Hussein!

CHAPTER 26

SADDAM OR BE DAMNED

*'If I took the job in Iraq, my boss would be
Saddam Hussein!'*

After Bernd Stange moved on from Oman, he landed the post as coach of Iraq, and it wasn't long before he got in touch to say he wanted me to come and be his goalkeeping coach. The one little snag, as far as I could see, was that Saddam Hussein was still ruling the roost in Iraq at the time and his eldest son Uday was in charge of the football federation. Effectively, if I went there, my boss would be Saddam Hussein – and more immediately I'd be working for Uday, who had an even worse reputation than Saddam!

I had already heard all the stories in the aftermath of the 2002 World Cup about Saudi Arabia's players returning home in disgrace and having their faces slapped in public as a punishment because they had lost 8-0 to Germany. But being slapped was nothing compared to the stories you heard coming out of Iraq if their players had underperformed or returned from a particularly bad tournament. We heard that Uday had put some of his players in stocks before thrashing their feet with a cane. There was even talk of players being shot. There were also rumours about what went on within the football stadium in Iraq. The story went that because it was the biggest outdoor venue in the country, Saddam would use it get as many people as possible to come to his rallies, where he could rant and rave like Hitler. I was told that he actually used to take women who were accused of committing adultery out onto the pitch at half-time and have them shot in the goalmouth.

But Bernd insisted there was absolutely nothing to worry about. Because the war on Iraq was kicking off at the time, for safety reasons the Iraq football team could no longer train and play in their home country, and were based most of the time in neutral countries like Jordan. Bernd pushed and pushed and got the Iraqi FA – with both Saddam and Uday's names appearing on the top of the letterhead – to send me a written offer of $200,000 a year to be their goalkeeping coach.

At first, I turned it down flat because of all the scare stories that I heard. But Bernd was quite upset that I had dismissed it out if hand and kept on at me, assuring me it wasn't bad and insisting that the threat of any violence had been lifted. My head had been full of all these rumours about executions and players getting whipped, and I naturally thought to myself: 'What if one of my keepers makes a howler? I could get marched out of the dressing room and shot in the head!'

Bernd kept ringing me, urging me to keep an open mind, and eventually I thought 'sod it' and agreed to come to Baghdad and listen to what Uday had to say. This sounds crazy, but one of the reasons I went was because I had always wanted to go there since I was a kid, because I used to watch the old film *The Thief of Bagdad*!

The plane I travelled on to Iraq was unbelievable. There was only one flight a week from the region to Baghdad, so it was the only one I could get. It was meant to be first class, but it was an old converted Russian cargo plane, and I was one of only five or six passengers on board. When we got into the air, I went down the back of the plane and I couldn't believe what I saw. It was like a flying department store. There were kitchen sinks, car wheels, and a whole load of luxury items like shoes and salad cream – it was rammed full of stuff Iraqis couldn't get because of the sanctions against their country.

When I arrived, I was taken to a palace in Baghdad and given an amazing room. I only stayed the one night there, which was a pity, because it was old and ornate and obviously had a lot of history. The next day I was taken to another building and formally introduced to Uday, and even though I only spoke with him for 10 or15 minutes, he had immaculate English and came across as a nice guy. He didn't seem cruel at all, although I know that you can't judge someone by a brief meeting and I'm now aware of what he was capable of and his reputation as a butcher. I would have loved to have met Saddam as well, but funnily enough he was keeping a low profile at the time!

I went back to Oman and politely declined the job, but I would have liked to have worked for Iraq on a purely football basis because they had some magic players. I actually told Kevin Keegan when he was at Manchester City to sign a player called Nashat Akram. The kid was absolutely first class and he went on trial at City. He passed all the tests and Kevin wanted to sign him, but the British government wouldn't give him a work permit. He had great tricks, could run box to box, was full of energy and could score goals. He played under Steve McClaren at Twente in Holland, and has 100 caps for Iraq now, but it's a shame he wasn't allowed to come to England because he would have been a star in the Premier League.

Without the benefit of my expertise, Bernd didn't do too

badly for himself with Iraq. He's now coach of Belarus, and we stay in touch. Uday was less fortunate. He was hunted down and killed in a bunker by the Americans. When the FBI posted their list of most wanted war criminals, rating them by playing cards, Uday was rated as the Ace of Hearts. Now that more is known about his reign of terror, I can see he might not have been the best man to get on the wrong side of. According to the Iraq national team's Wikipedia page: 'Under Uday's leadership, motivational lectures to the team included threats to cut off players' legs, while missed practices resulted in prison time and losses resulted in flogging with electric cable or baths in raw sewage, if penalties or an open goal was missed or own goals were scored then that person would have their feet whipped with thorns.' It doesn't mention what happened to goalkeeping coaches but I'm mighty relieved I didn't get to find out.

I didn't really have to take the job in Iraq anyway, because when I'm not coaching I don't just sit about on my arse. I need to be busy all the time and I've been lucky enough to land some regular work as a television pundit.

The media work is always great fun. I've had the odd bit of stick for what I've said, but I'm not one for sitting on the fence and if you get people talking about the show and a point that you've raised then that's surely what it's all about.

I started working for a Saudi station called ART (Arab Radio and Television Network) about six or seven years ago. It was the perfect way to keep up to date with English football, which has a massive audience over here. To get paid for sitting watching live Premier League games and having my say on them is nice work if you can get it. I also got a regular gig alongside Joe Morrison on StarHub's Football Channel, which is broadcast in Singapore, and a newspaper column for *The*

Age newspaper here in Oman. I keep myself very busy and it's nice being a local celeb.

I'm still working alongside Joe on Ten Sports (Taj Entertainment Network), which broadcasts right across Asia. I drive him totally nuts, but he loves me really – despite what he might say! I gave him one of the most uncomfortable experiences of his broadcasting career during a game we covered. I had turned up in a tight-fitting suit, which I called my 'Gimp Suit' – it looked smashing, but it wasn't the most practical thing to wear because by the time we'd been sitting under the studio lights for a few minutes, I was sweating buckets. The suit was getting wetter and wetter, and it started to look like PVC. I decided I had to take the suit off, so I watched the rest of the first half in my vest and pants. I was so engrossed in the game, I forgot how close we were to going live on air again, and when the producer popped his head round the door to give us our two-minute warning, I had to try to throw my suit back on as quickly as I could. But in my haste to strip off, the trousers had got all tangled and I couldn't get the bloody things back on! When we got the countdown – '5, 4, 3, 2, 1...and live' – I was sitting behind my desk in my old apple-catchers trying to pretend like nothing was up. Joe was shifting about uncomfortably as – ever the professional – he tried to get on with his job, presenting the show and leading the half-time analysis, but he said later that every time he looked over at me he'd catch a glimpse of me scratching my nuts! We're still going strong, and I always enjoy testing his professionalism to the limits!

We've had a lot of good guests in the studio, and it's always nice to catch up with friends from the past in English football when they are over in the Middle East. I remember one time Gary O'Reilly, the former Tottenham and Palace defender, was a guest. It was the first time he had been on the show, so I got together with Joe Morrison beforehand and hatched a wind-up. He told Gary I'd forgotten to take my medication and that I suffered from severe Tourette's syndrome and could potentially go loopy at any time during the live broadcast. Joe told him it had happened once or twice before and just to be professional and try and roll with it.

When Gary sat down, Joe and I pretended the cameras were rolling, and within seconds I started cranking up the volume of my voice and then twitching in my seat. You could see Gary tensing up, fearing an end to his own TV career. Joe asked him a question to him about the Champions League and then asked me what I thought. I put on my maddest face (and believe me, it is a mad one) and said: 'Why don't you just go and fuck off!' I then stood up and started rocking the set, calling everyone bastards and shoving anyone who came my way. We got a couple of security guys to come and cart me away, and while Joe was trying to soothe Gary, I was still effing and blinding from the corridor. When I came back, we carried on and did the rest of the programme – with the cameras actually rolling this time – but Gary was a bag of nerves thinking I was going to kick off again. When we showed it to him later he took it well enough, although he called us a 'bunch of bastards' for stitching him up. Gary's done well for himself as a broadcaster, though, and he probably just puts the day I went loopy down to experience now!

I asked Joe to contribute a few choice words for this book of mine, and he said: 'Budgie and I have fought with the Afghans during a "friendly" game in Safa Park, we have played together alongside the Arabs on the beach at sunset in Oman, driven through the desert night talking shite about football and spent thousands of hours arguing about the Premier League in Studio One.

BUDGIE

'I don't believe he was a great goalkeeper (despite what he says), he is certainly not a great pundit (despite what he says) and he is absolutely not a great comedian (despite what he says) but he is a great character and he is great TV. Life needs colourful characters like Budgie and I believe that in football, as in television, the real characters are all disappearing. He is one of the last!'

I managed to cause quite a stir during my weekly appearances on StarHub, especially with my dress sense. For a game between Arsenal and Manchester United I wore a yellow jacket over a bright pink shirt, and the local paper described me as a 'camp European game-show host'.

It didn't bother me in the slightest. I took it as a compliment – I like to stand out from the crowd, as you might have gathered. 'If you think I'm outrageous now, I've got more clothes in my wardrobe that would really make an impact – black leather suits and white ones with pink braids,' I told the newspaper when they did an interview demanding to know what was on my clothes hangers at home. 'I'm imploring StarHub to let me loose. Take the chains off me and let me wear what I want! I'd wear my catsuit, the leopard-skin suit. The bright orange leather one. With nothing underneath. Football is an entertaining game. People want to see entertainment. And television is visual, it's about impact. I'm built like Tarzan – 95kg of sheer muscle. I'd take my shirt off.'

CHAPTER 27

OMAN IN THE GLOAMING

*'I would have won more than 100 caps for England
had I been a strapping six-footer! I didn't do badly
for myself, though, considering that in goalkeeping
terms at least, I am a bit of a shortarse.'*

After the battle to get back to fitness after my bicycle accident, life has been good again and I love it here in the Middle East. I live just beside the Indian Ocean. Janet and I own three houses in Oman, two within a new golf course complex plus a big cliff-top villa.

For anyone who doesn't know where Oman is, it's about a three-and-a-half hour drive from Dubai. Everyone has heard of Dubai now, but not everyone has heard of Muscat. I may be sounding like a representative for the Oman tourist board, but for me there is no contest – I'm in one of the most stunning places in the world. If you went straight across the Indian Ocean as the crow flies, you would be in Goa in India.

Millions of pounds are spent advertising the United Arab Emirates, Bahrain, Dubai and Abu Dhabi and Qatar, but take it from someone who lives here – there is only one naturally beautiful Gulf state and that is Oman. We have the mountains, the ocean and a picturesque city. The rest of the Gulf is mainly sand and desert, but here is very different and everyone is far more laid back. It's also got everything that Dubai has, albeit on a smaller scale.

People think that you can't drink in the Gulf, but let me educate you – that's a lot of bullshit. There's one or two places where you can't drink – like Saudi Arabia and Kuwait – but places like Oman, Bahrain, UAE and Qatar are as open as Britain. You can go and have a drink at any time. There are no pubs as such, as all the bars are contained within hotels, but they are nice and relaxed. There's more of a café culture here and everything is a bit more relaxed. There isn't anywhere near the level of drunkenness you see in Britain and, because of that, the crime rate is low. I can leave my car unlocked and not have to worry about it. You see guys heading to the beach for a kickabout after work instead of heading straight down to the pub. It's all nice and laid back.

Sitting in my hammock watching the waves of the Indian Ocean rolling by, it's impossible to say that I miss England and what the last few governments have let it become. When you earn £3,000 a week in England they'll take half off you in tax. I don't begrudge paying some tax, but the last time I was in England I had a problem with a couple of teeth I had damaged in my accident. One of my caps had fallen out and it would have been a 10-minute job to fix. But when I went to the surgery in Blackpool, they wouldn't help me out, giving me all the 'Are you registered, sir?' nonsense. I tried to tell them I'd paid millions of pounds in tax and played football for 32 years, but they weren't having it. It bugged me, because there were people strolling in there who hadn't paid one penny of tax.

It's the rip-off nature of Britain that bugs me too. I drive a Hummer and if I went to a British petrol station it would cost me about £170 to fill it bottom to top. In the Middle East, it costs me £15 at the most to fill it. In Britain, you work your balls off to earn a good salary and you get nothing back, but the government let anyone into the country and give them a house, free NHS and so on. The whole place is screwed up now. Me and Janet would never even think about going back. Sometimes I've flown back to Manchester, then got a train to Blackpool, and you see that the trains and stations are still like Victorian times, with people smoking and drinking their heads off on the trains. No wonder England's skint. It's full of freeloaders. I think it's down to the politicians, and it's wrong that people found guilty of fixing their expenses are still allowed to make the rules!

As you can see, I enjoy a good rant! I'll never be too old to climb up on my soapbox and shout the odds. But, in all seriousness, I rarely miss Britain and I'm better off where I am now, with the sun on my back every day. I still keep as fit as I can, and still have the same 32-inch waist and 46-inch chest I had when I was playing. When I had my Oman job I worked maybe 60 days a year with the national team and the age group teams, and perhaps most importantly I've rediscovered my love of football and going to matches. I've come a long way from the headcase that was bundled into the Priory. I've got the odd regret about decisions I took in my football career, but there's no point dwelling on them. My main regret is that I wasn't two inches taller – I would have won more than 100 caps for England had I been a strapping six-footer! I didn't do badly for myself, though, considering that in goalkeeping terms at least, I am a bit of a shortarse.

My position within the Oman national team allowed me to visit places I can't even spell! I've been to Uzbekistan, Tajikistan, Turkmenistan, Kathmandu, all over India and China, Korea, Japan, Sri Lanka, Australia, Malaysia,

Mongolia, Iraq and Iran – places that are so interesting and where you can learn so much. You wouldn't believe how many countries play football in Asia, and there are some bloody great players across the continent.

I honestly believe that in the next 20 years, an Asian country like India will be taking over football – just wait and see. I always believe in looking ahead, and in the future you will see Indians playing in the Premier League. They will also be running the Premier League too, because there are more billionaires there than anywhere else in the world. I think it's only a matter of time. China may yet emerge as a football superpower too. It's a myth in England that people in China are small – are they hell! The goalkeeper is six foot six and they are a big solid side. People underestimate Asian football at their peril. After the rubbish I watched from England at the World Cup in South Africa I have to say that India, Saudi Arabia and India would all give them a game.

These teams are to be particularly feared in their home stadiums – some of those grounds are frightening and volatile, to the extent that not only are you worrying about your safety, you're actually worrying about your life. Once you've been to the Azadi Stadium in Tehran in front of 120,000 fanatical supporters, anywhere else would be a walk in the park. I bet you Iran would beat England if they played them in the Azadi. People talk about Barcelona and Real Madrid being hostile places to go – you come to the Azadi and you'll find out what hostile really means. You wouldn't be able to see your hand in front of your face for the smoke and firecrackers.

It bugs me all the media hype about players like John Terry, who to me is nothing better than average. I've played with far better players than Terry. People should take a break from all the hype surrounding the Premier League and think more about what the rest of the world has to offer. There are a lot of players here in Asia who could very easily play in the Premier League, they just need to be discovered and given the chance. I brought over Ali Al-Habsi but there are countless more players in Asia that could make the grade.

I'm trying to bring the Middle East to the forefront of people's minds. People think they all drive around in luxury cars, that's rubbish, there are some tough areas too – and as we know from the success of Brazil and Argentina, that's often where you discover the best players because they are born with that gene that enables them to show the desire and hunger to fight their way to the top.

Sadly, my dream job with Oman was taken away from me by the national FA in January 2011. I'm still bitter about it, because I've done a hell of a lot for football in the country and they've sacked me for mistakes made by someone else. Claude Le Roy was the coach, and because they wanted him to go, they decided they wanted rid of everyone to do with him. It was harsh on him, too, because he won Oman the Gulf Cup in 2009, beating a lot of bigger nations along the way. That raised the bar, I suppose, and when we failed to qualify for the Asian Cup in 2011, they felt the team was underachieving. Oman are ambitious, and I can't fault them for that, but I do feel that they overreacted by giving us all the boot.

An interview I gave to *Gulf News* in September 2010, in which I called for backroom teams to be kept on and not be made to carry the can for the head coach, unfortunately fell on deaf ears. I said: 'If you have a good doctor, physio, coach or masseur – keep him – sack the head coach. Hire and fire independently. Then when it comes to appointments, a coach should only bring his own assistants. Other than that, the backroom staff should remain. Fitness coaches, goalkeeping coaches and assistants do most of the work in training – but they're losing their jobs because the head coach isn't up to it when it comes to matches.

'When a coach brings in his own people some of them are pizza delivery men who are brought in to keep the coach company with cups of coffee down the mall while they wait for training – staff and coach shouldn't be friends, they should just be good at their jobs. They're laughing all the way to the bank, taking clubs to the cleaners, walking out with big compensation packages, and I doubt the majority could produce professional coaching licences if asked.'

Sadly, Oman didn't see it that way, and because Claude was sacked, we all got punished, regardless of the service we had given to the FA and what we could still offer the country. It's so short-sighted. *Gulf News* phoned me after the sackings and I told them: 'I've done nothing wrong. In fact I've done more than anyone else in the Gulf; I've produced a phenomenon that's bigger than a Gulf Cup win. I'm very disappointed to have done so much for Oman, only to be treated in such a manner. I'm down in the dumps.'

I'm not down in the dumps now, though – life goes on, eh?

Football in the Middle East will come under the spotlight more and more in the next decade following FIFA's decision to give Qatar the 2022 World Cup, but to be brutally honest I think it's a disgrace to have it there. Qatar may be filthy rich, but at the moment the place is like a village. Having Zinedine Zidane to front the bid obviously helped their cause, but it just doesn't seem right to have it there. If it's held at the height of summertime, they would have to stage it indoors, in fully air-conditioned stadiums. They would have to build eight 60,000-seater stadiums. There is enough money to do that in Qatar, but it would be a massive break from tradition. The sensible option, if they insist on playing it there, is to move the World Cup to the winter.

I actually met the president of FIFA, Sepp Blatter, for the first time not long after Qatar won their World Cup bid. He had come to the Gulf to do some schmoozing, and visited Oman. He was touring our stadium and he saw that I had 'JB' on my Omani training kit. He looked me up and down and pointed to my initials, and said: 'JB? Joseph Blatter?' I replied: 'Ha-ha, pleased to meet you. My name is Bond…James Bond!'

I daresay Qatar will deliver the World Cup, because the country is so rich it's unbelievable. They already have brilliant indoor football fields, although to build enough stadiums to properly host a World Cup is a different matter. Their training ground reeks of money. Manchester United's training ground at Carrington is the best I have seen, but the one they have built in Qatar makes United's look old-fashioned!

Qatar may be ready for 2022, because of the money they have to prop up their bid, but I'm still scratching my head in disbelief that the biggest sporting event on the planet is heading there – it is such a small country. The capital, Doha, is the size of a small Scottish city, so it's basically like holding a world cup in Motherwell or Aberdeen! What I think they should have done is have one stadium here in Oman, one in Bahrain, one in UAE, Abu Dhabi and Dubai and make it a Gulf World Cup, but then I suppose you would be creating a new problem because the hosts usually qualify automatically. The bottom line is it's just too hot in the summer here. People would get sunstroke – the players and supporters. It's the desert, for God's sake. The best thing to do would be to share it around and hold the World Cup around Christmas time. It would be perfect conditions.

So, I don't necessarily agree with them holding it in Qatar, but the good thing is it will put the Gulf and football here firmly on the map. I hope to be there of course, and if the British teams happen to be there, be sure to look me up. I'll be the good-looking one that's still chirping away like a Budgie...

CHAPTER 28

HOW OTHERS SEE ME

*'I'm dreading the day he has to pack it all up – I
think he'd sooner have his heart taken out.'*
JANET BURRIDGE

O ver the years, my eccentricities and behaviour have
generated a few thousand column inches in newspapers,
magazines, fanzines, football programmes and autobiographies.
Some of them sound a bit too crazy to be true – but believe me
they are! I've also been touched to read some of the tributes and
fans' memories that are floating around cyberspace on the net,
and I am proud that a Facebook page has been set up by fans in
my honour. Everyone seems to have their say about me, and
here's a selection of my favourites from over the years...

JANET BURRIDGE
(Interviewed towards end of Budgie's playing career, 1997)

He twitches, fidgets and relives every moment of a game. He
grabs at imaginary shots, sets himself ready to spring for a corner
ball and yells warnings to defenders. I'm used to it. He's just so
energised when he's watching or replaying a game in his mind's

eye, he just can't keep still. He was watching a match in bed one night. I'd fallen asleep as I was dead tired after a day in our sportswear shop. But he woke me, made me sit up and was shouting: 'Watch this! Look at the keeper, he's sold himself. Sold, sold, sold himself! What do you think of that?' He made me watch the slow motions three times until I said I knew what he was talking about. I didn't really, but it kept him quiet.

Once when we were sleeping, he hit me with his elbow. And when I woke him up he couldn't believe it. He said he was going up for a ball – at least that was his excuse. I'm dreading the day he has to pack it all up – I think he'd sooner have his heart taken out.

When he plays he has terribly desolate moments, even if his side has won 5-1. The fact that he has let in even one goal leaves him devastated. If he's made just one mistake, he is inconsolable. But whatever happens, he is either going through the game in his sleep, pushing shots over the bar and waving his arms about, or sitting bolt upright saying to me: 'It's all right, love, someone just hit a tremendous shot at me.'

Even when he's watching a game on telly, his body starts to sway and his eyes are elsewhere, in a penalty area somewhere, and we can see his fingers getting ready to grab a shot. He ends up in a hell of a state. I've even heard him give an interview to BBC television in his sleep. But he's such a No.1 optimist he just got himself all fired up again and bounced back – mostly in his sleep, of course.

(Interviewed in 2011)

Coming to the end of his playing career was an event so devastating to John that it is hard for many to comprehend. Once he started to cope a little with not crossing that white line at 3pm on a Saturday afternoon, he knew he still had his physical fitness, which he worked on meticulously 'just in case he was needed in the Premier League'. But then the accident that would have killed most people took that away too.

His zest for the game has never wavered, whether it is a park game or a cup final. Wearing gloves to watch a game on TV was his way of living through the game as if he was in goal. He would wear his boots to make sure they were match fit and totally comfortable, like a second skin. He would say 'Fail to prepare, prepare to fail'. The equipment he took with him onto the pitch was cared for with the utmost reverence – I wouldn't dream of going near his kit! It never went into the team kit skips, nor was it ever left at the ground. Throughout my 40 years of knowing John I have heard others say that different players are dedicated, but let me tell you, not one has ever come anywhere close to John. He lived football 100% of the time and that has never changed.

His love for the game is infectious. When we moved to Oman he realised a dream, that of playing beach football every evening just like on the Copa Cabana. I remember the first night he went down to play he was like a little boy, wondering if he could get a game! After a week he was upgraded to another team, then after a while he came home with the biggest grin on his face telling me he had been first pick! For a beach game! Whichever team John played on (strangely enough he never played in goal) would win. He used to go down to the beach an hour or so before the game to prepare the 'pitch', even having special goals hand made. Yes, I am talking about a 50-year-old who played over 1000 top-flight games. I could go on forever!

STEVE HARPER
(Newcastle United goalkeeper, 1993–present)

If you are not brave then you cannot play in goal. It is all part of the job. I can remember on my first day as a professional in 1993 John Burridge screaming at me, saying I had to taste blood running down my neck. Budgie was a cracker who used to encourage forwards to go in on our keepers, but he was a huge influence on my career in my first two years.

TIM FLOWERS
(Team-mate at Wolves and Southampton)

Enjoying football, whatever the result, and having a rapport with the fans, are two of the many things I learned from Budgie. My style is totally different to Budgie's because I'm a different shape and a different person. But when we were at Wolves together and again at Southampton he always put in 100 per cent, which is what I try to do.

ALAN SHEARER
(Team-mate at Southampton)

I often used to join Budgie and a few others in small-sided matches after regular training. On one occasion I chased a through ball and he went down at my feet, so I jumped over him to avoid a nasty collision. Budgie stood up, stopped the game and said: 'Look, son, when a goalkeeper dives at your feet he expects you to clatter him. Don't disappoint him.' I got the message straight away. It was John's way of suggesting I had to develop a ruthless streak. A few years later in a friendly match between Southampton and Falkirk, Budgie was in goal for the Scottish club. During the game he threw himself at my feet to smother the ball, I followed through, caught him on the head and split it open, leaving a wound which required three stitches. Budgie wiped away the blood and came over to me. I was half expecting him to have a go at me, but he patted me on the head and said: 'Well done, son, I'm proud of you.'

NIGEL MARTYN
(Protégé at Leeds United)

Budgie has helped improve every aspect of my game. He's very passionate about football. The word mad comes to mind. But he comes to see me at Leeds from Blyth, and gives me the intensive work I need. And if I do well on a Saturday, he'll ring me up that night and tell me. If things go wrong, I'd rather discuss things with him than go away on my own.

ALI AL-HABSI
(First Oman player to play in the English Premier League, with Bolton and Wigan)

Budgie came to England with me, because I was a 17-year-old from a village team and everything was so new for me. No one imagined a Middle East footballer would ever play in the Premier League. Like many other players I had dreamed of that, but never believed it would come true. While I was here Budgie took me to Old Trafford, and he could see I was wide-eyed and overawed by being there. He said: 'If you work hard and fulfil your potential you will play here one day.' But when it actually happened, I could still hardly believe it. If it wasn't for John's help and what he taught me about goalkeeping, the dream wouldn't have come true.

BUDGIE

ASHLEY HAMMOND
(Local reporter, friend and failed Budgie agent, Oman and UAE 2006–2011)

To me, Budgie was just a face on the back of one of my football cards and a passing reference in various players' memoirs as the fruit-loop that walked on his hands, wore gloves to bed and got his wife to throw oranges around the room at him. When I met him in one of my first assignments as a young reporter in Muscat, Oman, working on a local paper there in 2006, he was to instantly mean much more than that – not a day has passed since where I haven't had at least ten missed calls from him before seven in the morning. He affectionately dubbed me 'Harry Harris' or 'Clark Kent, the mild-mannered reporter'.

One image of Budgie that still plagues me was when we travelled from Muscat to London to watch Ali Al-Habsi make his Bolton debut in the League Cup against Fulham, a game the Wanderers won 2-1. Ali had played a blinder and afterwards John and myself ran to the bottom right of the Putney End to congratulate Ali. John had tears rolling down his face and was attempting to jump the barrier, shouting, voice croaking, 'That's my boy, that's my boy,' as he was held back by stewards. Ali walked into the Cottage oblivious – just out of earshot to Budgie being apprehended by the orange army. That, for me, typified the sort of thankless situation Budgie often found himself in. He still looked a prat even in that poignant memory, though, with a fluffy Biggles leather aviator's hat and goggles on with floppy dog ears covering his lugs.

DAVID HARDIE
(Hibs football writer, *Edinburgh Evening News*)

Budgie probably embodied the saying that to be a goalkeeper you also need to be a bit mad. Eccentric without doubt, a character both on and off the field but also an exceptional goalkeeper, one who enjoyed a lengthy and varied career thanks not only to his undoubted ability between the sticks but his slavish attention to fitness.

He may have drawn more than a few laughs from his team-mates when he'd roll up for training at Wardie on that tiny moped on which he completed the final couple of miles from his home in the north of England after arriving by train at Waverley each day, but once the gloves were on it was down to business as the young goalkeepers at Easter Road at the time soon realised.

Chris Reid, Stephen Woods and Jason Gardiner, who were all born AFTER Budgie had made his League debut for Newport County in 1969, presented him with a cake to mark his 40th birthday a few months after he'd helped Hibs lift the Skol Cup, all three admitting they were left simply in awe of the punishing workout he'd put himself through before returning home for another 90 minutes in the gym.

Like any goalkeeper Budgie was strong-willed and determined with an unshakeable belief in his own ability, once famously claiming: 'Peter Shilton? I wouldn't let him keep my pigeons.'

DAVID HARRISON
(Writing in Wolves' matchday magazine)

I was a frequent visitor to the Burridge household when he was a Wolves player from 1982–84. 'Just pop round for a chat and a bit to eat' was the regular invite. The evenings were never

BUDGIE

dull. Tales of Budgie's madcap methods were already legendary. I was once told that when he was at Aston Villa his neighbours were alarmed one night when they heard a constant thumping noise from next door. On further examination, they found Budgie jumping from his garage roof. He was working on his agility and landing techniques.

If you get the impression that he was slightly eccentric, you are wrong. He was mad. Barking mad.

But he was also a consummate professional. There was method in his madness. He maintained the highest level of fitness of any footballer I have known. To have played for 29 clubs in 771 games over a period of 30 years he must have been doing something right.

TIM NASH
(Football writer, *Wolverhampton Express and Star*)

As a young Wolves fan of 12 in the summer of 1983, I attended training sessions at Wolverhampton & Bilston Athletic Club, based at Aldersley Stadium, two miles from Molineux. I was amazed to discover, on looking at a mass football match going on in an adjoining field, Budgie playing outfield. There may have been up to 15-a-side playing, and Budgie was throwing himself around the pitch, albeit in what would have been the closed season!

MARTIN HAWORTH
(Durham City fan)

He spent the entire 90 minutes of each game coaching the back four. You would imagine that for someone who has played at the very highest level that he wouldn't really be bothered with football at this level, but his enthusiasm really was infectious. He played for Durham in a friendly against Sunderland, and again he was a joy to watch. When Durham were stuck again for a keeper in September, John was unavailable because of his contract with Blyth Spartans, but he arranged for one of the youth team keepers at Leeds United to turn out for Durham, ferrying the lad to and from the lad's Hull home for the two games we needed him. The man is an absolute diamond, and as mad as a hatter.

PHIL DAVISON
(Enfield fan)

When he played for Enfield, he once travelled down south to catch the team coach back to the north-east for Bishop Auckland v Enfield (FA Trophy) because he said it was good for team morale (it was!). Rumour has it that when Enfield signed him, the chairman wasn't too sure about having a goalie older than he was so Budgie proved his fitness by diving over the boardroom table three times. He never let in a goal in a league match for Enfield before the lure of Aberdeen became too much for him.

ANDY BIRD
('Budgie the Legend' Facebook page)

I saw Newcastle win away at Brighton 3-0 in 1989/90. It was totally out of the blue as we were totally rubbish at the time, John's reaction after the game was like we'd won the European Cup and he practically climbed into the away end. Total and utter legend. Respect.

APPENDIX

CAREER STATISTICS

HONOURS

1971
Anglo-Italian Cup winner
12 June: Bologna 1, Blackpool 2 (after extra time)
(Stadio Renato Dall'Ara, Bologna)

1972
Anglo-Italian Cup runner-up
24 June: Roma 3, Blackpool 1
(Stadio Olimpico, Rome)

1977
League Cup winner
12 March: Aston Villa 0, Everton 0 (Wembley)
16 March: Aston Villa 1, Everton 1 (Hillsborough, after extra time)

13 April: Aston Villa 3, Everton 2 (Old Trafford, after extra time)

1978/79
Second Division Champions: Crystal Palace

1982/83
Second Division runners-up: Wolves

1991
Skol League Cup winner
27 October: Hibernian 2, Dunfermline 0 (Hampden)

1996
Inducted into Blackpool Hall of Fame

CAREER STATS

Year	Club	Appearances
1969–1971	Workington	27
1971–1975	Blackpool	134
1975–1978	Aston Villa	65
1978	Southend United (loan)	6
1978–1980	Crystal Palace	88
1980–1982	Queens Park Rangers	39
1982–1984	Wolverhampton Wanderers	74
1984	Derby County (loan)	6
1984–1987	Sheffield United	109
1987–1989	Southampton	62
1989–1991	Newcastle United	67
1991–1993	Hibernian	65

BUDGIE

Year	Club	Appearances
1993	Newcastle United (reserve keeper)	
1993	Scarborough	3
1993–1994	Lincoln City	4
1994	Enfield	0
1994	Aberdeen	3
1994	Newcastle United	0
1994	Dunfermline Athletic	0
1994	Dumbarton	3
1994	Falkirk	3
1994–1995	Manchester City	4
1995	Notts County	0
1995	Witton Albion	0
1995	Darlington	3
1995–1996	Grimsby Town	0
1996	Gateshead	0
1996	Northampton Town	0
1996	Queen of the South	6
1996	Purfleet	0
1996	Blyth Spartans	0
1996	Scarborough	0
1997	Blyth Spartans	0

Total appearances (not including friendlies and non-league matches): 771